JUDO FOR EVERYONE

JUDO FOR EVERYONE

NOT JUST FOR THE ATHLETICALLY INCLINED

SID KELLY
8TH DAN JUDO

Order this book online at www.trafford.com
or email orders@trafford.com

Most Trafford titles are also available at major online book retailers.

Print information available on the last page.

ISBN: 978-1-4907-9682-6 (sc)
ISBN: 978-1-4907-9683-3 (e)

Trafford rev. 08/19/2019

North America & international
toll-free: 1 888 232 4444 (USA & Canada)
fax: 812 355 4082

This book is dedicated to the late Bill Myers (4th Dan) who sadly passed away December 2018. He was one of the first to regularly use the Five Steps to Randori with his beginner's classes at Cornell University Judo Club, where, as he once quoted, they went from zero to competent and confident randori in three months, not knowing they were doing randori. To them it was just an extension of the drills they were practicing.

CONTENTS

INTRODUCTION

It wasn't that long ago that lots of people smoked in the US. Whole families smoked while the kids watched and waited for their turn to come around. Rich and poor smoked. Friends smoked. Movie stars smoked. Movies were inundated with cool movie stars elegantly holding cigarettes and smoothly inhaling and exhaling smoke. Fast forward to today and now hardly anyone smokes in the US. After people became informed things changed. Women fought for hundreds of years for the right to vote. Men thought women were too emotional and incapable of making logical decisions. Even some women didn't think women should vote; Florence Nightingale was one. Work that one out? Fast forward to today and no one questions a women's right to vote. After people became informed things changed.

Many other things were staunchly accepted in their time: slavery, blood-letting, and lack of hygiene in hospitals, to name a few. In each case all these things were accepted by the experts of the day. And in each case trying to change them was tenaciously fought against to maintain the status quo. Then a trickle of understanding turned into a flood, and after the light of reason prevailed, the thing being fought against was accepted.

In the above examples, people at the time thought nothing was wrong with the way things were being done. Could it be that such things are happening and have always happened in judo? Are there things that everyone does, and previous generations have done since the founding of judo that could be improved upon? If judo is such a wonderful thing, why aren't the phones ringing off the hook? If everything is fine with the way judo is taught why do so many people leave? If everything is fine with the way judo is taught why is the US judo population around 20,000 or so where the US yoga population is around 35,000,000? Is it the subject matter itself, (liking or disliking throwing and being thrown — one example) or is it how the subject matter is presented to the public, (randori without prior preparation — one example) that is the cause of why the judo population is so small?

Regarding the title, 'Judo for Everyone.' It literally means this is about everyone who enrolls in judo classes. Those that enroll are hoping to find something that is fun, and challenging, all within their limits, that they are able or willing to try. This book attempts to show that judo has great appeal to only a small number of people (especially the athletically inclined) because of the way judo is now introduced and practiced. Because of this, the book suggests ways of making judo more interesting for everyone who gives judo a try — judo for everyone.

Regarding, 'There's No regurgitated Judo Here.' The dictionary defines regurgitating as repeating information without analyzing or comprehending it. Here no old information is being repeated to analyze or comprehend. This book has nothing to do with what is usually found in judo books, eg, — techniques — kuzushi, etc. Everything here is fresh judo food for thought.

While bearing the above historical facts in mind (smoking, women's emancipation, and others) it is hoped that the reader, when reflecting on ideas in this book, will wonder, is there something staring me in the face that I can't see which is negatively influencing judo? If h/she does, I hope h/she finds it.

COMPARING JUDO

WITH

OTHER SPORTS

COMPARING JUDO TO OTHER SPORTS

INTRODUCTION

As far as the American Public is concerned judo doesn't exist because they never see or hear anything about it. Although some well-established annual contests still exist: the NY Open International, the Liberty bell PA, and others. Some thirty years ago Connecticut used to host a tournament every two or three weeks, now there is only two tournaments a year! Today there are a few classes here and there and judo die-hards occasionally get together and discuss the good old days. But in the good old days judo never had any competition. There was no Bruce Lee, Gracie Ju-jitsu and MMA using modern marketing techniques. Instead, the judo community plodded along, year in year out, doing the same old things (kata - randori - shiai). They never tried to popularize judo using any form of mass marketing. They thought the good days would last forever. And as we know, they didn't. Some other facts to consider from all this are: If judo is such a marvelous pastime why doesn't the American public show some interest in it? Why didn't a healthy size of the judo population continue on down from the good old days? If judo is such a wonderful pas-time, why is it most beginners leave before they hardly get warmed up to the ways of judo? To answer these questions, it will be informative to first look at what other sports have to offer, especially where beginners are concerned. Below is a chart with five groups of sports along with their five methods of scoring.

SPORTS AND THEIR METHODS OF SCORING

No	EXAMPLES OF SPORT OR ACTIVITY	METHOD OF SCORING
1	Running - Swimming - Cycling - Snow-boarding - Skiing	Time
2	Long jump - High jump - Javelin - Shot-putting - Archery Weight-lifting - Discus	Distance
3	Dancing - Diving - Ice-skating - Gymnastics - Synchronized-swimming	Aesthetics
4	Tennis - Volley-ball - Baseball - Soccer - Basket-ball - Table-Tennis - Ice-hockey - Boxing - Karate	Projected Skills
5	Greco-Roman-wrestling - High-school-wrestling - Judo Sumo	Wrestling Skills

THE REASONS WHY

1) Consider from a beginners point of view, scoring based on time.
    All beginners can run. But many beginners cannot swim, cycle, snow-board and ski. But they can learn to. *Then they can practice and have fun unhampered and unobstructed by the actions of others.*

2) Consider from a beginners point of view, scoring based on distance.
    All beginners can long-jump, high-jump, throw a javelin and discus, shot-put, lift weights and fire an arrow. *They can practice and have fun unhampered and unobstructed by the actions of others.*

3) Consider from a beginners point of view, scoring based on aesthetics.
    Beginners cannot dance, dive, ice-skate, know any gymnastics or synchronized swimming. But they can learn to. *Then they can practice and have fun unhampered and unobstructed by the actions of others.*

4) Consider from a beginners point of view, scoring based on projected skills.
    Most beginners already have the skills to play tennis, volley-ball, baseball, soccer, basketball, and table-tennis. *They can practice and have fun unhampered and unobstructed by the actions of others.* Most beginners need to learn how to skate to play ice-hockey, and need to learn some punches and kicks to be able to box and practice karate. *Then they can practice and have fun unhampered and unobstructed by the actions of others.*

5) Consider from a judo beginners point of view, scoring based on wrestling (wrestling as a verb) skills.
    Beginners can easily learn judo throwing and grappling techniques. With grappling beginners can have fun, even though they are hampered and obstructed by the close contact of others. *But most beginners cannot find much fun practicing standing randori. They are hampered and obstructed to such a high degree that they can hardly try any throwing techniques.* There is no enjoyment or satisfaction in this. (Remember, we are referring to beginners). They become frustrated and leave in large numbers before realizing the wonderful benefits that judo has to offer.

In plain English, standing randori is far too difficult for most beginners compared to the introductory activities of other recreational pastimes. What is needed to change this judo conundrum is a brand new, refreshing, revolutionary method of introducing standing randori to beginners, and additional user friendly types of randori and contests for beginners, and recreational players.

ANALYZING

JUDO'S

CATEGORIES

JUDO FOR EVERYONE

BEFORE CONSIDERING WAYS TO MAKE JUDO MORE USER FRIENDLY FOR EVERYONE IT WILL BE BENEFICIAL TO FIRST CONSIDER WHAT THE PUBLIC ARE PRESENTLY OFFERED WHEN THEY SIGN UP FOR JUDO CLASSES

THE BASIC CATEGORIES OF JUDO

FOR THOSE THAT STAY THE COURSE THE ABOVE BASIC CATEGORIES OF JUDO WORK VERY WELL FOR THE FOLLOWING:

1)   THE ATHLETICALLY INCLINED.

2)   THE VERY INTERESTED.

3)   THE VERY PATIENT.

SEE PAGE 10 REGARDING THE RESULTS FOR THE MAJORITY OF PEOPLE WHO GIVE JUDO A TRY

JUDO FOR EVERYONE

THE BASIC CATEGORIES OF JUDO

BECAUSE OF THE ABRUPT TRANSITION FROM KATA TO
RANDORI, AND THE UNCLEAR BOUNDERIES OF RANDORI
INTENSITY, THE THREE CATEGORIES DO NOT WORK WELL
FOR MOST PEOPLE.

THEIR CONTINUED USE AS THE TEACHING TOOLS OF JUDO IS
ONE OF THE REASONS WHY JUDO IS IN SUCH RAPID DECLINE
IN THE USA AND WHY JUDO IS NOT AS POPULAR AS IT USED TO
BE IN OTHER PARTS OF THE WORLD.

EACH CATEGORY WILL NOW BE REVIEWED,
HIGHLIGHTING THEIR PROBLEMS ALONG WITH
SUGGESTED SOLUTIONS. SEE PAGES 11 TO 20.

JUDO FOR EVERYONE
(THE KATA CHART)

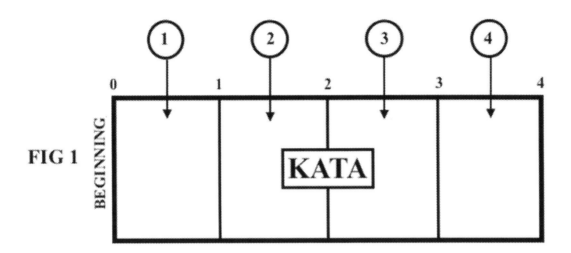

FIG 1

1) **LEARNING TECHNIQUES:**
   *Breakfalls - *Throws - *Avoidances - Holds - Chokes - Arm locks.

2) **SOLO:**
   Breakfalls - Miming Techniques.

3) **INFORMAL:**
   Uchi-komi - Breakfalls - Drills (Tachi-waza and Newaza)
   *Floating Drills

4) **FORMAL:**
   The Traditional Seven Katas - New Formal Katas.

WHAT ARE THE PROBLEMS HERE?

There are no problems here. Most people when beginning judo easily adjust to learning techniques. Applying them is a different story. See fig 2 - page 12.

* Learned for the 5 Steps to Randori — page 41

11

JUDO FOR EVERYONE
(ANALYZING KATA TO RANDORI)

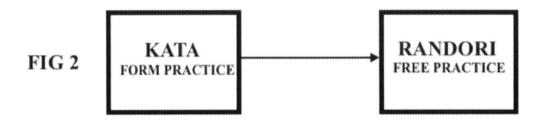

FIG 2

WHAT ARE THE PROBLEMS HERE?

1) There is no transitional connection between Kata and Randori.
   In kata partners cooperate and in randori they don't.

2) Beginners are not prepared for the competitive skills needed to practice
   randori (competitive is not referring to randori as a competition but as
   a means of developing and improving skills). Just knowing techniques —
   throws and breakfalls — are not skills needed for randori. Skills are: free
   floating movements, timing, distance judgement, a sense of feel, and more.

3) Beginners become frustrated and disillusioned with randori and drop out.

FOR A SOLUTION — SEE Page 13 - Fig 3

JUDO FOR EVERYONE
(A NEW CATEGORY)

A SOLUTION

KATA	KADORI	RANDORI
FORM PRACTICE	RANDORI PREPARATION	FREE PRACTICE

FIG 3

There needs to be a new category — an interim stage between kata and randori that prepares beginners for randori. This new category was named KADORI.

KADORI = KATA + RANDORI

Kadori is neither kata or randori — Kadori is a bit of both It's the bridge between kata and randori.

For complete details regarding KADORI see page 85

See Page 14 - Fig 4 for the KADORI chart

JUDO FOR EVERYONE
(THE KADORI CHART)

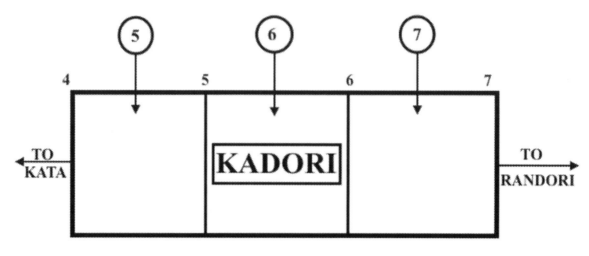

FIG 4

5)　**STING DRILLS:**
Sting Drills are an extension of the Floating Drills learned in kata. They consist of one throw and an avoidance defense. They are identical in form to the Floating Drills except they are competitively applied. This is the beginning of the gradual introduction of non cooperation between partners.

6)　**THE BULL AND THE MATADOR:**
The Bull and the Matador combines three sting drills. Using three throws one partner tries to throw the other while the other defends using only avoidance defenses. As in a bull fight the defender (the matador) allows, even encourages, the bull (the attacker) to attack so the matador can display his defending skills.

7)　**FLOATING RANDORI:**
Floating Randori extends the Bull and the Matador one step further. Both attack and both defend. Both are bulls and both are matadors. Both do not restrict the other's attacks and both only defend by avoiding, and not blocking attacks.

FOR PROBLEMS WHEN PRACTICING RANDORI SEE Page 15 - Fig 5

JUDO FOR EVERYONE
(ANALYZING RANDORI)

TO
KADORI

RANDORI

TO
SHIAI

FIG 5

WHAT'S THE PROBLEM HERE?

The problem here is students are only given one type of randori to enjoy and train with. It is only when two practitioners are equally matched and practicing with equal intensity is there an equal playing field. Because the present type of randori ranges from practicing light to extremely intense each persons desired level of practice intensity is unlikely to coincide with the other practitioner (a different playing field). As each practitioner is different, regarding, experience, fitness, strength, desires, emotions and size, the problem of finding a common practicing boundary with the one type of randori is elusive and the cause of much frustration. So much so many people leave judo before they give themselves enough time to adjust and enjoy the practice of randori.

FOR A RANDORI SOLUTION SEE THE RANDORI CHART
Page 16 - Fig 6

JUDO FOR EVERYONE
(THE RANDORI CHART)

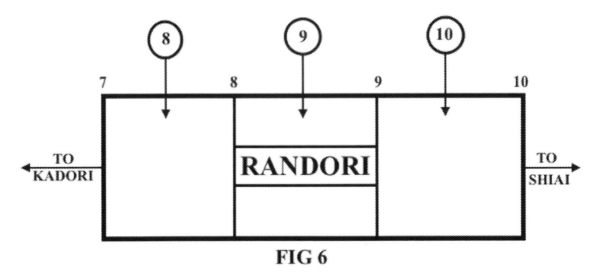

FIG 6

A SOLUTION

A solution is made available by having three types of randori. The difference between each randori style is its method of defense: See below.

8) FLOATING RANDORI (KADORI)
Floating Randori is free practice randori with ONLY tai-sabaki type avoidance defenses allowed. It is the last of the Kadori exercises.

9) REGULAR RANDORI (FREE PRACTICE)
Regular standing randori is the ideal learning exercise. But it requires both partners to allow attacks to happen, while preventing throws from happening by tai-sabaki avoidances, and hip reaction blocking. (By constantly blocking throwing attacks with stiff arms skill development is constantly blocked).

10) CONTEST RANDORI (SHIDORI)
Contest randori is as the title suggests; attacking and defending within the contest rules of the IJF. It's all give and no take randori.

FOR CONTEST PROBLEMS SEE Page 17 - Fig 7

JUDO FOR EVERYONE
(ANALYZING SHIAI)

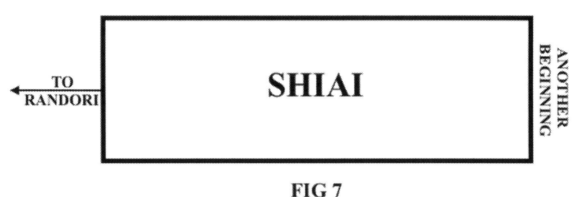

FIG 7

WHAT'S THE PROBLEM HERE?

The problem here is students are only given one type of contest to enjoy and train with. Naturally a contest is supposed to be difficult. It's judo's ultimate challenge. But there is no style of contest designed for intermediate players, or people who have been practicing judo for a long time (aging recreational players) who are not interested any more in striving to be the best they can be at contest. Also owing to the restrictive nature of judo (two people interlocked) many people drop out of judo before they give themselves enough time to adjust to the ways of the present one type of shiai.

FOR A SHIAI SOLUTION SEE THE SHIAI CHART
Page 18 - Fig 8

JUDO FOR EVERYONE
(THE SHIAI CHART)

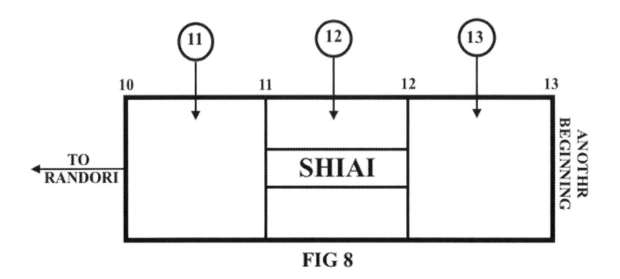

FIG 8

A SOLUTION

A solution is made available by having three types of contest. The difference between each type of contest is its method of defense: See below.

11) **BEGINNERS CONTEST:**
Beginners Contest is Floating Randori in the form of a contest where only avoidance defenses are allowed to prevent being thrown. See Beginners Contest Rules — Page 120.

12) **RECREATIONAL CONTEST:**
Recreational Contest is Regular Randori in the form of a contest where only avoidance defenses and reaction hip blocking are allowed to prevent being thrown. See Recreation Contest Rules — Page 124.

13) **SHIAI (THE ULTIMATE CONTEST):**
The Ultimate Contest is the standard shiai as is now practiced today.

FOR THE TOTAL SOLUTION OF CATEGORIES SEE Page 19 - Fig 9

JUDO FOR EVERYONE
(PUTTING THE CATEGORIES TOGETHER)

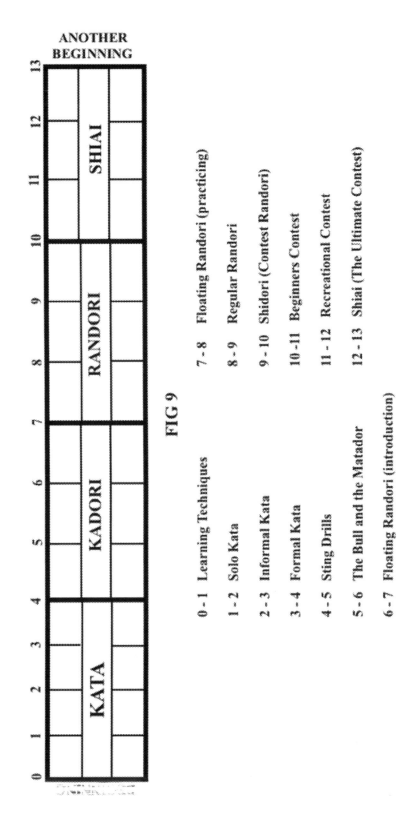

FIG 9

0 - 1   Learning Techniques

1 - 2   Solo Kata

2 - 3   Informal Kata

3 - 4   Formal Kata

4 - 5   Sting Drills

5 - 6   The Bull and the Matador

6 - 7   Floating Randori (introduction)

7 - 8   Floating Randori (practicing)

8 - 9   Regular Randori

9 - 10 Shidori (Contest Randori)

10-11   Beginners Contest

11 - 12 Recreational Contest

12 - 13 Shiai (The Ultimate Contest)

JUDO FOR EVERYONE
(PREPARATION CHART — FIG 10)

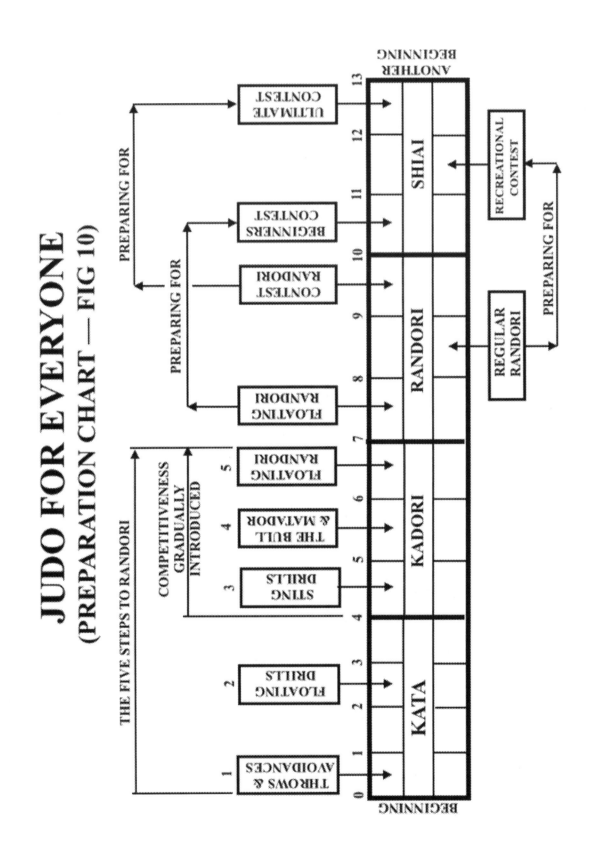

JUDO FOR EVERYONE
(SUMMARY —FIG 11)

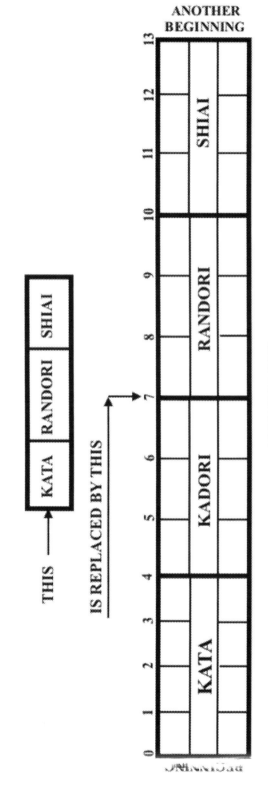

THIS ——→ | KATA | RANDORI | SHIAI |

IS REPLACED BY THIS

ANOTHER BEGINNING

| 0 | 1 | 2 | 3 | 4 | 5 | 6 | 7 | 8 | 9 | 10 | 11 | 12 | 13 |

KATA   KADORI   RANDORI   SHIAI

ADVANTAGES

1) Gradual introduction to the competitive skills of randori.

2) Students are introduced to judo first and fighting second. Not as now, fighting first and judo second.

3) Three choices of randori.

4) Three choices of contest.

5) Each type of contest has its own randori preparation.

6) Because the system is more user friendly there will be less drop out.

DISADVANTAGES
A SLOWER START BUT A MUCH BETTER FINISH

SUMMARY
OF
ANALYSIS

In this section it was shown, or tried to show, that judo is not for everyone with what the present system offers. The present system does not prepare beginners for randori. Learning break falls and throws are not the skills needed for standing randori — they are only its end use: break-falling for uke, and throwing for tori. The present system only offers the public, and recreational players who wish to remain practicing judo, one type of randori and one type of shiai. The system works well for those that are athletically inclined and are still able to enjoy the rigors of judo, and for those, for whatever reason, have been drawn to and have developed a strong interest in judo.

The essential problems are:

1) Technique form (throws and break-falls) are not randori skills.
2) Randori has no guideline boundaries.
3) Contest is too demanding for most people.

BEGINNERS AND INTERMEDIATE PLAYERS RANDORI PROBLEMS

For the beginner there is no system available that prepares h/her for randori. H/she is just thrown in cold turkey, which more often than not is the result of h/her being thrown out (they don't stay). This also applies to intermediate players who still haven't adjusted to the rigors of randori. The five steps to randori is a solution to the problem. Through a series of five steps a beginner is gradually introduced to the competitive nature of randori along with the elementary skills needed to randori: free floating movements, timing, distance judgement, feel, and most important of all, knowing that randori practice is about US not ME. But even with the advantages of being versed in the five steps to randori the beginner, and the intermediate player, will still be confronted with a contest type randori (shidori). Learning how to contest is not part of the five steps because the five steps is about introducing the art aspects not the martial aspects of judo. So can beginners and intermediate players, without prior preparation for randori, whether the storms of rigorous randori? Some do but most don't. Some leave quickly and others gradually. Hence the need for another randori between the lighter Floating Randori and the strenuous Contest Randori — Regular Randori. Regular Randori is more challenging than Floating Randori because of the addition of reactive hip blocking, but nowhere near as challenging as Contest Randori where the hands and arms can constantly block throwing attacks.

23

AGING PLAYERS RANDORI PROBLEMS

Here aging refers to anyone who is past h/her physical prime; whether it is someone who tries judo later in life or is an aging recreational player who is unable to practice with the same vigor h/she used to. Besides physical limitations a major problem is often not wanting to admit h/she is not up to it (hard randori) any more. Given enough time nature takes care of this. You just can't do it anymore. But in the meanwhile, h/she has to practice with younger players who have no idea how tired the older more skillful person may be. The aging player has to make some decisions, stay or leave. Often the adjustment is made by practicing with persons of the same age. But as these numbers decrease randori practice no longer has the appeal it once had.

THE SOLUTION

The solution is to have three distinct different types of randori.
1) Floating Randori:
   a) For beginners who are just introduced to randori.
   b) For intermediate players who have not yet adapted to the rigors of contest randori, or have, but do not wish to practice contest randori.
   c) For contest players who wish to improve pure judo skills by using only avoidance defenses.

2) Regular randori:
   a) For intermediate players who have not yet adapted to the rigors of contest randori, or have, but do not wish to practice contest randori.
   b) For experienced recreational players who no longer wish to practice contest randori.
   c) For contest players who wish to improve their judo skills by using only avoidance defenses and reactionary hip blocking defenses.

3) Contest Randori (Shidori)
   a) For contest players who wish to improve their contest skills or are preparing for an upcoming contest
   b) For anyone who gets satisfaction from practicing all out — at whatever level.

These three types of randori each have strict boundaries (their methods of defending) that makes them distinct and separate from one another. The three types of randori are shown on pages 16 & 20. For beginners and intermediate players who were not introduced to randori with the five steps, and for aging players who practice with a style that's contest oriented there will be a learning curve. Floating and Regular Randori with only avoidance and hip blocking defenses will take some getting used to. But it is these differences, or boundaries, that separates Floating and Regular Randori from what is now, more often than not, the randori norm — contest randori (shidori).

GOING NOWHERE

RANDORI

GOING NOWHERE RANDORI

BECAUSE BEGINNERS ARE NOT PREPARED FOR RANDORI IT IS PREDICTABLE WHAT TYPE OF STYLE THEY WILL DEVELOP — ONE OF STIFF ARMED FIGHTING — WHEN THEY FIRST PRACTICE AND CONTINUE TO PRACTICE RANDORI.

THERE ARE ALWAYS EXCEPTIONS BUT A SYSTEM MUST CATER FOR THE MANY — NOW IT DOESN'T.

THE FOLLOWING FLOW CHARTS CONVEY THE PATH OF THE EARLY YEARS OF RANDORI THAT IS GOING NOWHERE

GOING NOWHERE RANDORI

THE THREE CATEGORIES OF JUDO

| KATA | RANDORI | SHIAI |

% OF COMPETITION IN KATA - RANDORI - SHIAI

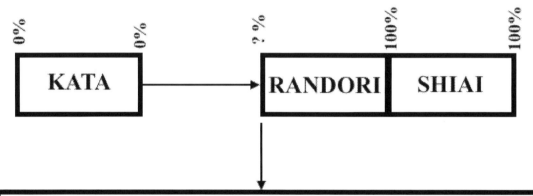

WHEN BEGINNER'S ATTEMPT STANDING RANDORI WITH ONLY SOME KATA EXPERIENCE THEY WILL NOT POSSESS ANY OF THE ELEMENTARY COMPETITIVE SKILLS NEEDED TO EXECUTE A THROW AGAINST A RESISTING PARTNER WHO, AT THE SAME TIME IS TRYING TO THROW HIM: SOME OF THESE SKILLS ARE: MANUEVERING - FEEL - TIMING - COPING WITH RESISTANCE - THROWING AND DEFENDING AWARENESS - TEMPO AND HARMONY. WITHOUT THESE COMPETITIVE SKILLS, BEGINNERS, FOR THE MOST PART, WILL PRACTICE A RANDORI THAT IS GOING NOWHERE, WHICH WILL MANIFEST ITSELF IN THE FOLLOWING WAYS:

SEE PAGE 29

GOING NOWHERE RANDORI

AFTER ONLY EXPERIENCING KATA - AND THEREFORE NO PREPARATION TO ADAPTING TO RESISTING FORCES - THE OUTCOME OF RANDORI IS USUALLY AS FOLLOWS ——

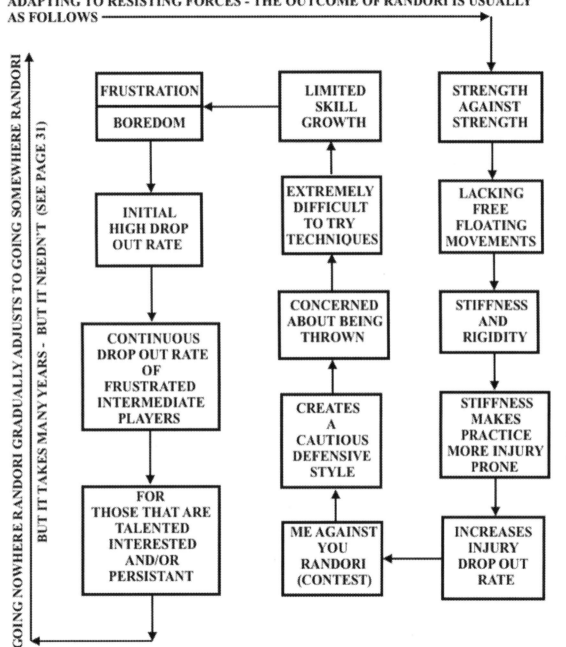

GOING NOWHERE RANDORI GRADUALLY ADJUSTS TO GOING SOMEWHERE RANDORI
BUT IT TAKES MANY YEARS - BUT IT NEEDN'T (SEE PAGE 31)

FRUSTRATION
BOREDOM

LIMITED SKILL GROWTH

STRENGTH AGAINST STRENGTH

INITIAL HIGH DROP OUT RATE

EXTREMELY DIFFICULT TO TRY TECHNIQUES

LACKING FREE FLOATING MOVEMENTS

CONTINUOUS DROP OUT RATE OF FRUSTRATED INTERMEDIATE PLAYERS

CONCERNED ABOUT BEING THROWN

STIFFNESS AND RIGIDITY

CREATES A CAUTIOUS DEFENSIVE STYLE

STIFFNESS MAKES PRACTICE MORE INJURY PRONE

FOR THOSE THAT ARE TALENTED INTERESTED AND/OR PERSISTANT

ME AGAINST YOU RANDORI (CONTEST)

INCREASES INJURY DROP OUT RATE

GOING

SOMEWHERE

RANDORI

GOING SOMEWHERE
RANDORI

AFTER BEGINNERS HAVE COMPLETED THE FIVE STEPS TO RANDORI INTRODUCTION IT IS PREDICTABLE WHAT TYPE OF STYLE THEY WILL BE PRACTICING — FREE FLOATING.

THE FOLLOWING FLOW CHARTS CONVEY THE PATH THEY WILL ENCOUNTER DURING THEIR RANDORI INTRODUCTORY PERIOD.

GOING SOMEWHERE RANDORI

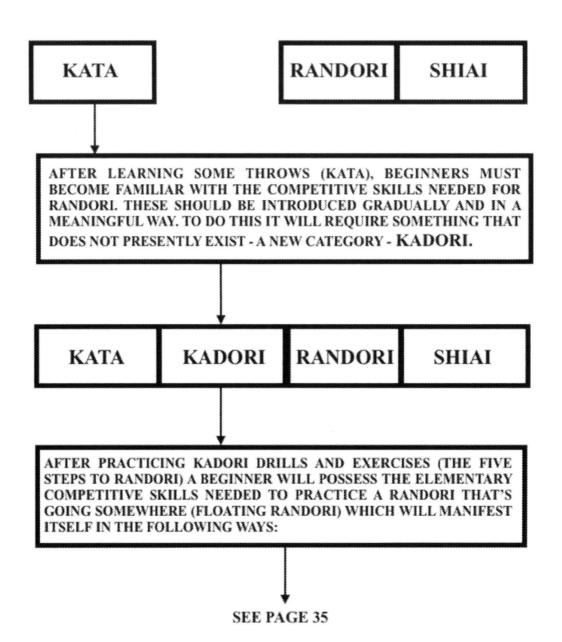

KATA

RANDORI	SHIAI

AFTER LEARNING SOME THROWS (KATA), BEGINNERS MUST BECOME FAMILIAR WITH THE COMPETITIVE SKILLS NEEDED FOR RANDORI. THESE SHOULD BE INTRODUCED GRADUALLY AND IN A MEANINGFUL WAY. TO DO THIS IT WILL REQUIRE SOMETHING THAT DOES NOT PRESENTLY EXIST - A NEW CATEGORY - **KADORI.**

KATA	KADORI	RANDORI	SHIAI

AFTER PRACTICING KADORI DRILLS AND EXERCISES (THE FIVE STEPS TO RANDORI) A BEGINNER WILL POSSESS THE ELEMENTARY COMPETITIVE SKILLS NEEDED TO PRACTICE A RANDORI THAT'S GOING SOMEWHERE (FLOATING RANDORI) WHICH WILL MANIFEST ITSELF IN THE FOLLOWING WAYS:

SEE PAGE 35

GOING SOMEWHERE RANDORI

THE OUTCOME OF THE KADORI FIVE STEPS IS USUALLY AS FOLLOWS

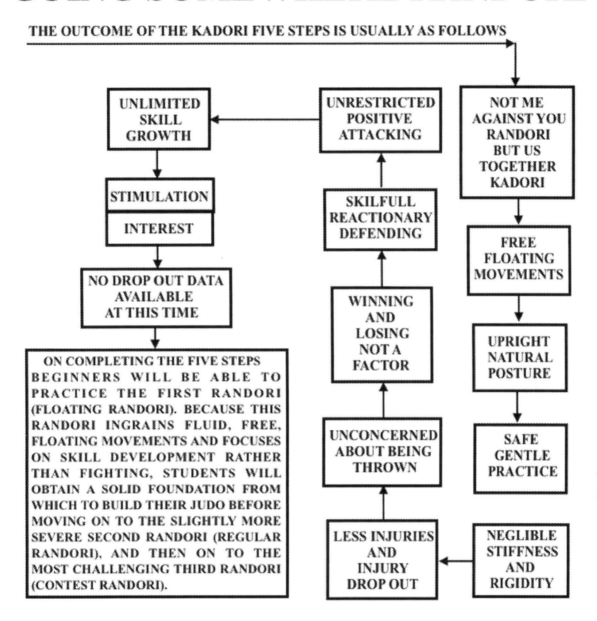

UNLIMITED SKILL GROWTH

UNRESTRICTED POSITIVE ATTACKING

NOT ME AGAINST YOU RANDORI BUT US TOGETHER KADORI

STIMULATION

INTEREST

SKILFULL REACTIONARY DEFENDING

FREE FLOATING MOVEMENTS

NO DROP OUT DATA AVAILABLE AT THIS TIME

WINNING AND LOSING NOT A FACTOR

UPRIGHT NATURAL POSTURE

ON COMPLETING THE FIVE STEPS BEGINNERS WILL BE ABLE TO PRACTICE THE FIRST RANDORI (FLOATING RANDORI). BECAUSE THIS RANDORI INGRAINS FLUID, FREE, FLOATING MOVEMENTS AND FOCUSES ON SKILL DEVELOPMENT RATHER THAN FIGHTING, STUDENTS WILL OBTAIN A SOLID FOUNDATION FROM WHICH TO BUILD THEIR JUDO BEFORE MOVING ON TO THE SLIGHTLY MORE SEVERE SECOND RANDORI (REGULAR RANDORI), AND THEN ON TO THE MOST CHALLENGING THIRD RANDORI (CONTEST RANDORI).

UNCONCERNED ABOUT BEING THROWN

SAFE GENTLE PRACTICE

LESS INJURIES AND INJURY DROP OUT

NEGLIBLE STIFFNESS AND RIGIDITY

THE FIVE STEPS

TO STANDING

RANDORI

STAGE 1

CONSISTING OF
THREE THROWS
AND AVOIDANCES

THE FIVE STEPS TO STANDING RANDORI
FIG 12

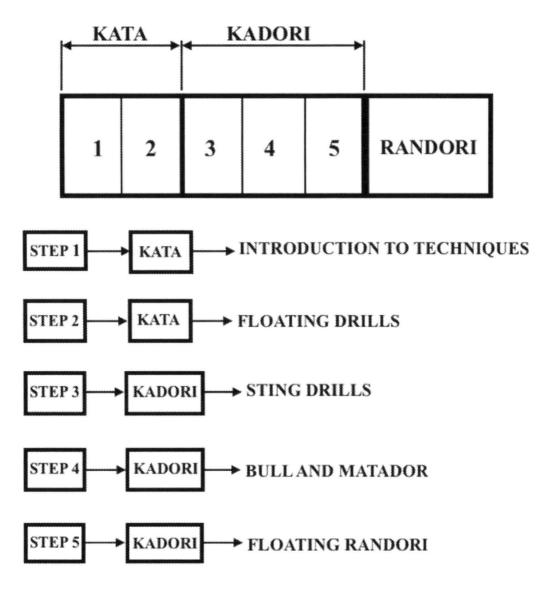

SEE YouTube — SID KELLY JUDO THE 5 STEPS

INTRODUCTION TO TECHNIQUES
STAGE 1 — STEP 1
FIG 13

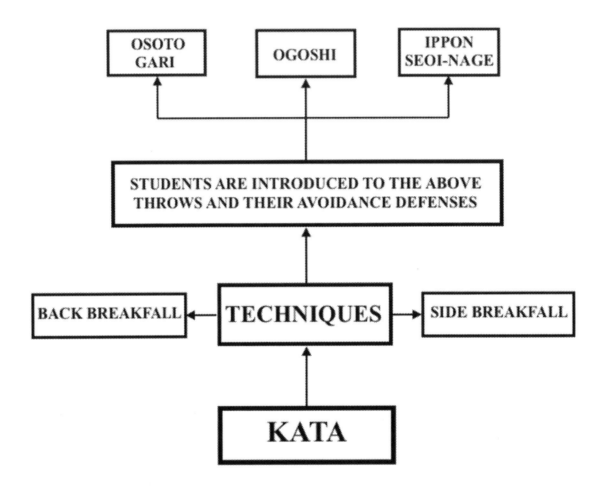

THE ROLLING BREAKFALL AND FRONT BREAKFALL ARE NOT TAUGHT OR NEEDED AT THIS STAGE.

FLOATING DRILLS
STAGE 1 — STEP 2
FIG 14

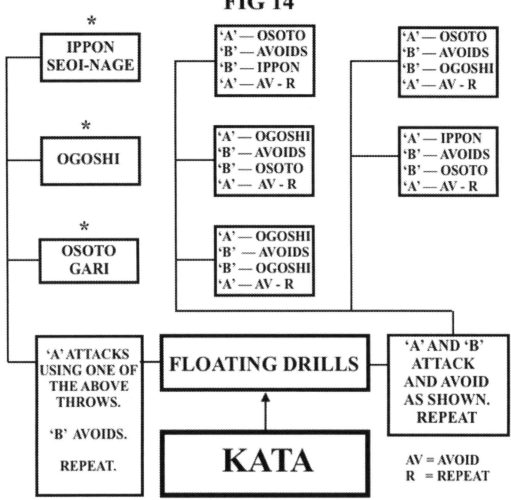

```
        *                ┌─────────────────┐      ┌─────────────────┐
  ┌─────────────┐        │ 'A' — OSOTO     │      │ 'A' — OSOTO     │
  │   IPPON     │        │ 'B' — AVOIDS    │      │ 'B' — AVOIDS    │
  │ SEOI-NAGE   │        │ 'B' — IPPON     │      │ 'B' — OGOSHI    │
  └─────────────┘        │ 'A' — AV - R    │      │ 'A' — AV - R    │
                         └─────────────────┘      └─────────────────┘
        *
  ┌─────────────┐        ┌─────────────────┐      ┌─────────────────┐
  │   OGOSHI    │        │ 'A' — OGOSHI    │      │ 'A' — IPPON     │
  └─────────────┘        │ 'B' — AVOIDS    │      │ 'B' — AVOIDS    │
                         │ 'B' — OSOTO     │      │ 'B' — OSOTO     │
                         │ 'A' — AV - R    │      │ 'A' — AV - R    │
        *                └─────────────────┘      └─────────────────┘
  ┌─────────────┐
  │   OSOTO     │        ┌─────────────────┐
  │   GARI      │        │ 'A' — OGOSHI    │
  └─────────────┘        │ 'B' — AVOIDS    │
                         │ 'B' — OGOSHI    │
                         │ 'A' — AV - R    │
                         └─────────────────┘
```

'A' ATTACKS USING ONE OF THE ABOVE THROWS.

'B' AVOIDS.

REPEAT.

FLOATING DRILLS

KATA

'A' AND 'B' ATTACK AND AVOID AS SHOWN. REPEAT

AV = AVOID
R = REPEAT

* THESE DRILLS ARE MANDATORY. STUDENTS MUST BE WELL VERSED IN THEIR AVOIDANCES. THE OTHER DRILLS SHOULD BE PRACTICED BUT NOT DWELLED UPON.

THERE IS NO THROWING IN THE KATA EXERCISE OF FLOATING DRILLS. HOWEVER, TORI MUST APPLY ENOUGH EFFORT WITH HIS THROWING ATTACKS SO UKE IS ABLE TO AVOID OR RIDE THE THROW USING TORI'S THROWING FORCES.

STING DRILLS
STAGE 1 — STEP 3
FIG 15

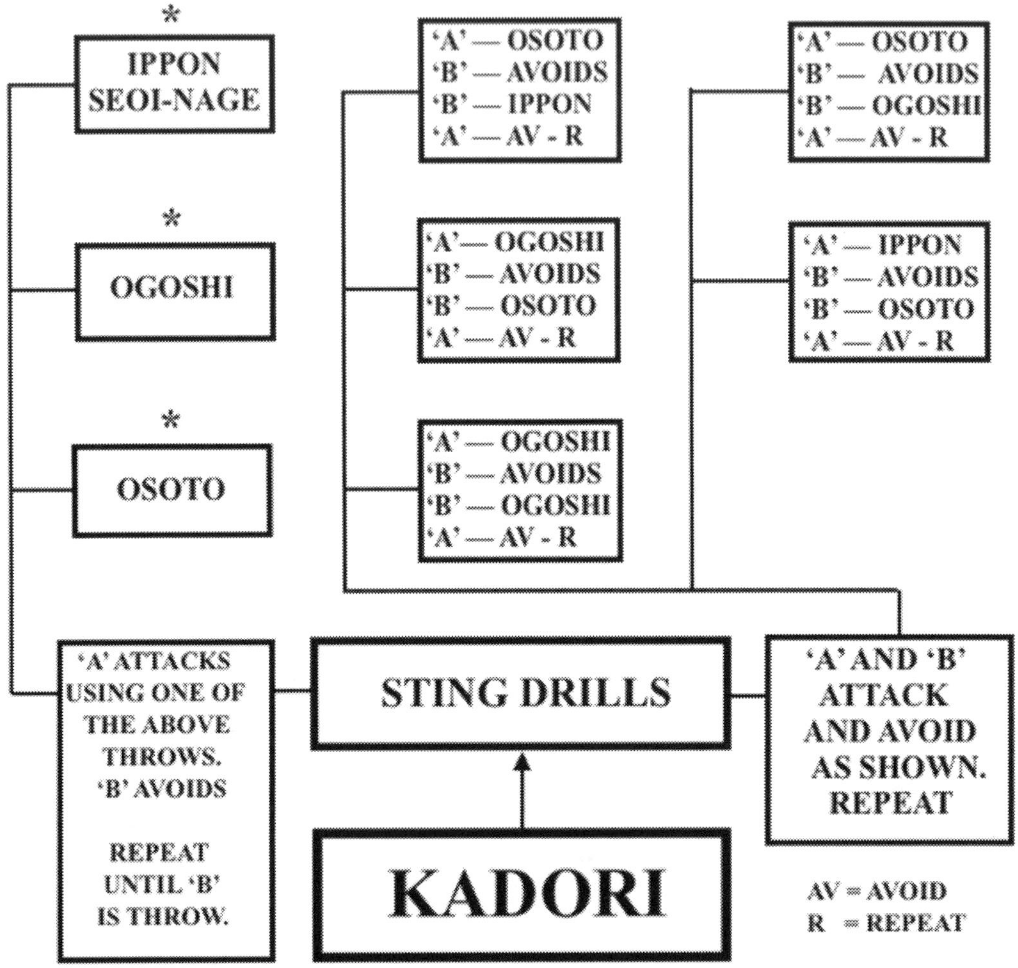

*

```
IPPON
SEOI-NAGE
```

*

```
OGOSHI
```

*

```
OSOTO
```

```
'A' — OSOTO
'B' — AVOIDS
'B' — IPPON
'A' — AV - R
```

```
'A' — OGOSHI
'B' — AVOIDS
'B' — OSOTO
'A' — AV - R
```

```
'A' — OGOSHI
'B' — AVOIDS
'B' — OGOSHI
'A' — AV - R
```

```
'A' — OSOTO
'B' — AVOIDS
'B' — OGOSHI
'A' — AV - R
```

```
'A' — IPPON
'B' — AVOIDS
'B' — OSOTO
'A' — AV - R
```

```
'A' ATTACKS
USING ONE OF
THE ABOVE
THROWS.
'B' AVOIDS

REPEAT
UNTIL 'B'
IS THROW.
```

```
STING DRILLS
```

```
'A' AND 'B'
ATTACK
AND AVOID
AS SHOWN.
REPEAT
```

```
KADORI
```

AV = AVOID
R = REPEAT

* THESE DRILLS ARE MANDATORY. STUDENTS MUST BE WELL VERSED IN THESE DRILLS. THE OTHER DRILLS SHOULD BE PRACTICED BUT NOT DWELLED UPON.

DURING THE KADORI STING DRILL EXERCISES THROWS ARE DILIGENTLY ATTEMPTED. DEFENDERS MAKE NOT THE SLIGHTEST EFFORT TO PREVENT ATTACKS. DEFENDERS EITHER AVOID AN ATTACK USING AN AVOIDANCE SKILL OR GET THROWN (THE STING).

THE BULL AND THE MATADOR
STAGE 1 — STEP 4
FIG 16

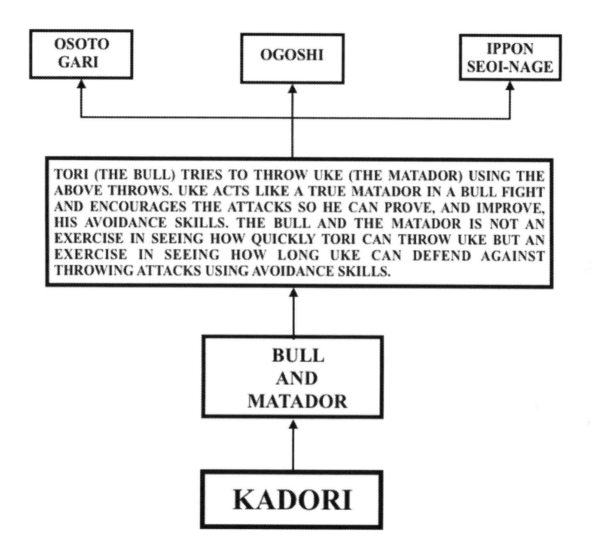

| OSOTO GARI | OGOSHI | IPPON SEOI-NAGE |

TORI (THE BULL) TRIES TO THROW UKE (THE MATADOR) USING THE ABOVE THROWS. UKE ACTS LIKE A TRUE MATADOR IN A BULL FIGHT AND ENCOURAGES THE ATTACKS SO HE CAN PROVE, AND IMPROVE, HIS AVOIDANCE SKILLS. THE BULL AND THE MATADOR IS NOT AN EXERCISE IN SEEING HOW QUICKLY TORI CAN THROW UKE BUT AN EXERCISE IN SEEING HOW LONG UKE CAN DEFEND AGAINST THROWING ATTACKS USING AVOIDANCE SKILLS.

BULL AND MATADOR

KADORI

THE BULL AND THE MATADOR IS THE COLLECTIVE PRACTICE OF ALL THE STING DRILLS

FLOATING RANDORI
STAGE 1 — STEP 5
FIG 17

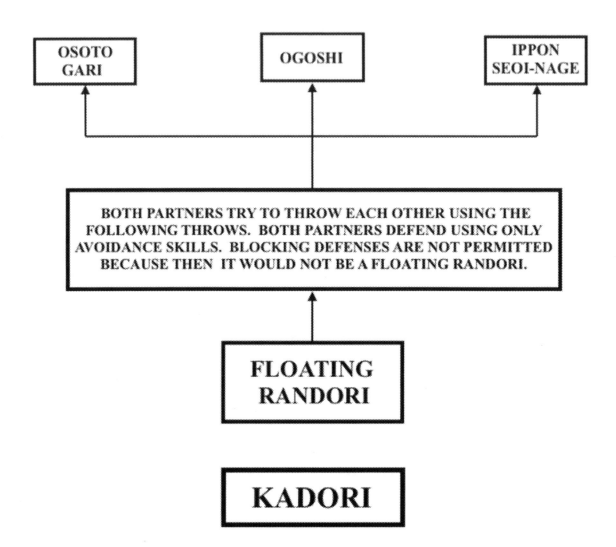

OSOTO GARI

OGOSHI

IPPON SEOI-NAGE

BOTH PARTNERS TRY TO THROW EACH OTHER USING THE FOLLOWING THROWS. BOTH PARTNERS DEFEND USING ONLY AVOIDANCE SKILLS. BLOCKING DEFENSES ARE NOT PERMITTED BECAUSE THEN IT WOULD NOT BE A FLOATING RANDORI.

FLOATING RANDORI

KADORI

FLOATING RANDORI IS A NATURAL EXTENSION OF THE BULL AND THE MATADOR

STAGE 2

CONSISTING OF
SEVEN THROWS
AND AVOIDANCES

INTRODUCTION TO TECHNIQUES
STAGE 2 — STEP 1
FIG 18

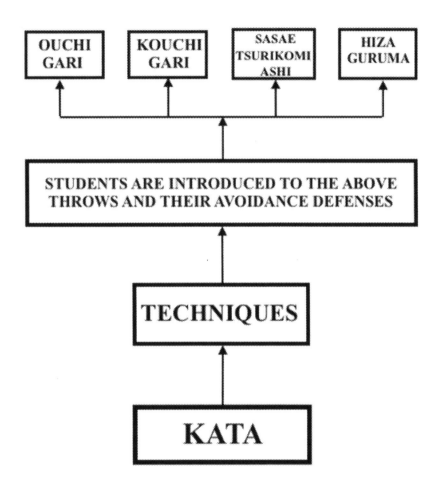

FLOATING DRILLS
STAGE 2 — STEP 2
FIG 19

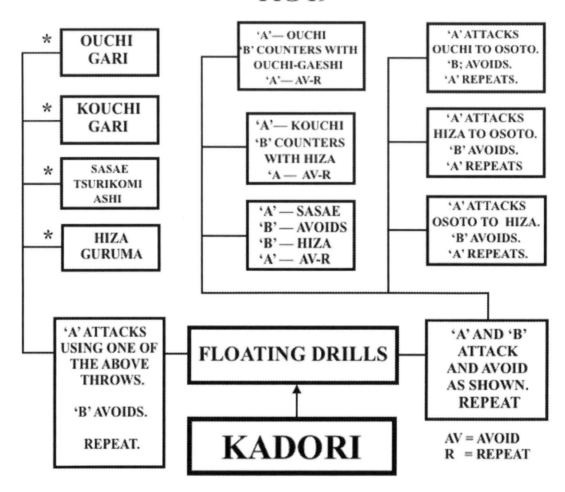

* OUCHI GARI	'A'— OUCHI 'B' COUNTERS WITH OUCHI-GAESHI 'A'— AV-R	'A' ATTACKS OUCHI TO OSOTO. 'B; AVOIDS. 'A' REPEATS.
* KOUCHI GARI	'A'— KOUCHI 'B' COUNTERS WITH HIZA 'A — AV-R	'A' ATTACKS HIZA TO OSOTO. 'B' AVOIDS. 'A' REPEATS
* SASAE TSURIKOMI ASHI	'A' — SASAE 'B' — AVOIDS 'B' — HIZA 'A' — AV-R	'A' ATTACKS OSOTO TO HIZA. 'B' AVOIDS. 'A' REPEATS.
* HIZA GURUMA		

'A' ATTACKS USING ONE OF THE ABOVE THROWS.

'B' AVOIDS.

REPEAT.

FLOATING DRILLS

KADORI

'A' AND 'B' ATTACK AND AVOID AS SHOWN. REPEAT

AV = AVOID
R = REPEAT

*THESE DRILLS ARE MANDATORY. STUDENTS MUST BE WELL VERSED IN THEIR AVOIDANCES. THE OTHER DRILLS SHOULD BE PRACTICED BUT NOT DWELLED UPON.

THERE IS NO THROWING IN THE KATA EXERCISE OF FLOATING DRILLS. HOWEVER, TORI MUST APPLY ENOUGH EFFORT WITH HIS THROWING ATTACKS SO UKE IS ABLE TOO AVOID OR RIDE THE THROW USING TORI'S THROWING FORCES.

STING DRILLS
STAGE 2 — STEP 3
FIG 20

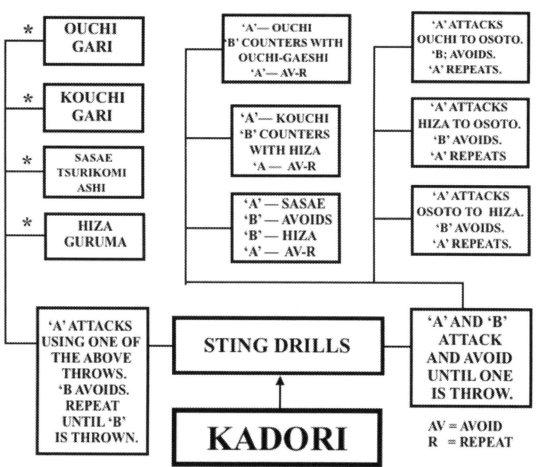

* THESE DRILLS ARE MANDATORY. STUDENTS MUST BE WELL VERSED IN THESE DRILLS. THE OTHER DRILLS SHOULD BE PRACTICED BUT NOT DWELLED UPON.

DURING THE KADORI STING DRILL EXERCISES THROWS ARE DILIGENTLY ATTEMPTED. DEFENDERS MAKE NOT THE SLIGHTEST EFFORT TO PREVENT ATTACKS. DEFENDERS EITHER AVOID AN ATTACK USING AN AVOIDANCE SKILL OR GET THROWN (THE STING).

THE BULL AND THE MATADOR
STAGE 2 — STEP 4
FIG 21

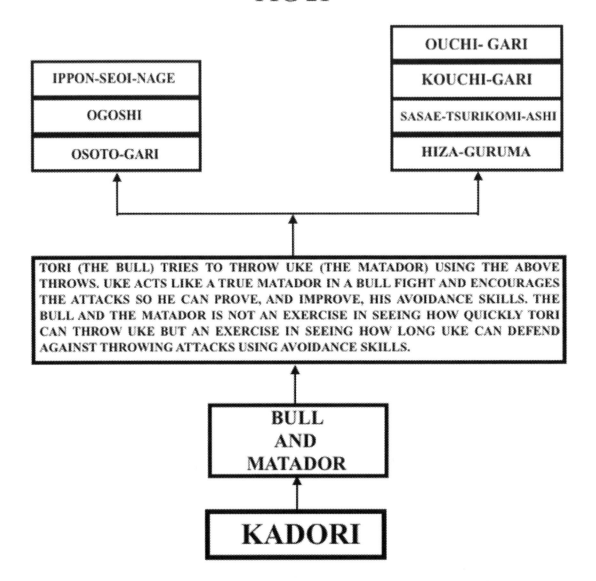

IPPON-SEOI-NAGE
OGOSHI
OSOTO-GARI

OUCHI- GARI
KOUCHI-GARI
SASAE-TSURIKOMI-ASHI
HIZA-GURUMA

TORI (THE BULL) TRIES TO THROW UKE (THE MATADOR) USING THE ABOVE THROWS. UKE ACTS LIKE A TRUE MATADOR IN A BULL FIGHT AND ENCOURAGES THE ATTACKS SO HE CAN PROVE, AND IMPROVE, HIS AVOIDANCE SKILLS. THE BULL AND THE MATADOR IS NOT AN EXERCISE IN SEEING HOW QUICKLY TORI CAN THROW UKE BUT AN EXERCISE IN SEEING HOW LONG UKE CAN DEFEND AGAINST THROWING ATTACKS USING AVOIDANCE SKILLS.

BULL AND MATADOR

KADORI

THE BULL AND THE MATADOR IS THE COLLECTIVE PRACTICE OF ALL THE STING DRILLS

FLOATING RANDORI
STAGE 2 — STEP 5
FIG 22

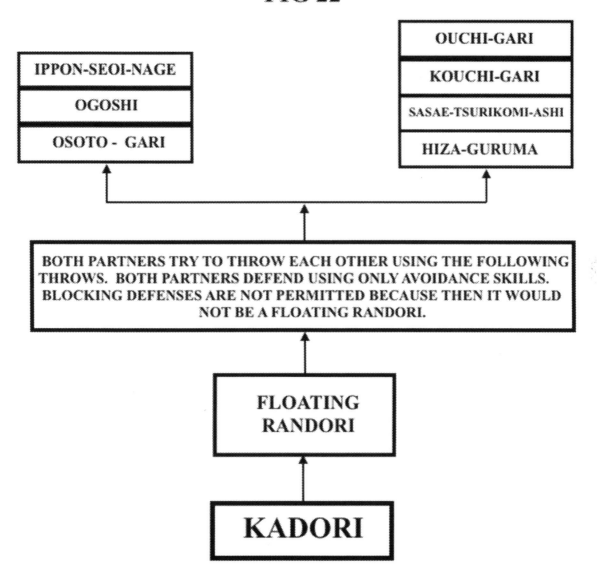

| IPPON-SEOI-NAGE |
| OGOSHI |
| OSOTO - GARI |

| OUCHI-GARI |
| KOUCHI-GARI |
| SASAE-TSURIKOMI-ASHI |
| HIZA-GURUMA |

BOTH PARTNERS TRY TO THROW EACH OTHER USING THE FOLLOWING
THROWS. BOTH PARTNERS DEFEND USING ONLY AVOIDANCE SKILLS.
BLOCKING DEFENSES ARE NOT PERMITTED BECAUSE THEN IT WOULD
NOT BE A FLOATING RANDORI.

FLOATING RANDORI

KADORI

FLOATING RANDORI IS A NATURAL EXTENSION OF
THE BULL AND THE MATADOR

STAGE 3

CONSISTING OF
TEN THROWS AND
AVOIDANCES

INTRODUCTION TO TECHNIQUES
STAGE 3 — STEP 1
FIG 23

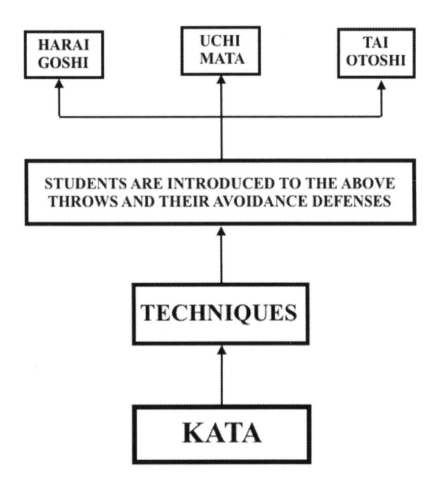

FLOATING DRILLS
STAGE 3 — STEP 2
FIG 24

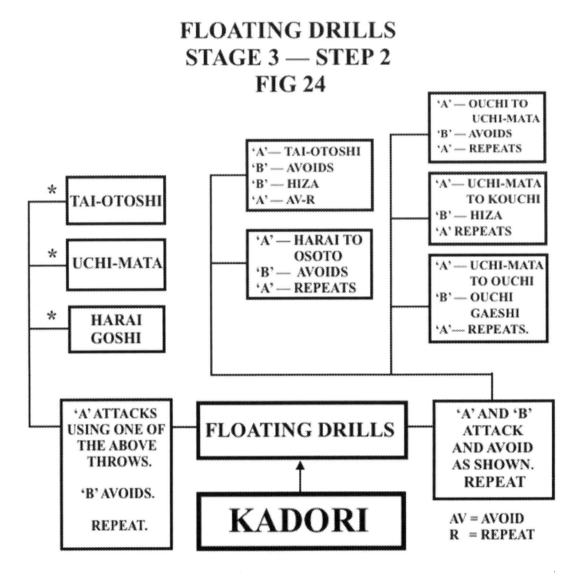

* THESE DRILLS ARE MANDATORY. STUDENTS MUST BE WELL VERSED IN THEIR AVOIDANCES. THE OTHER DRILLS SHOULD BE PRACTICED BUT NOT DWELLED UPON.

THERE IS NO THROWING IN THE KATA EXERCISE OF FLOATING DRILLS. HOWEVER, TORI MUST APPLY ENOUGH EFFORT WITH HIS THROWING ATTACKS SO UKE IS ABLE TOO AVOID OR RIDE THE THROW USING TORI'S THROWING FORCES.

STING DRILLS
STAGE 3 — STEP 3
FIG 25

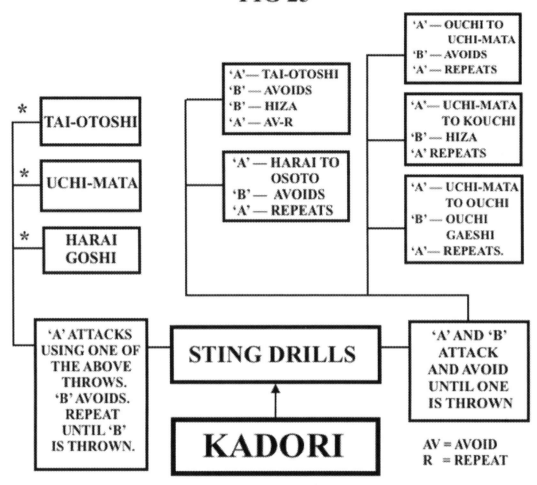

'A'— OUCHI TO
UCHI-MATA
'B'— AVOIDS
'A'— REPEATS

'A'— TAI-OTOSHI
'B'— AVOIDS
'B'— HIZA
'A'— AV-R

'A'— UCHI-MATA
TO KOUCHI
'B'— HIZA
'A' REPEATS

'A' — HARAI TO
OSOTO
'B'— AVOIDS
'A'— REPEATS

'A'— UCHI-MATA
TO OUCHI
'B'— OUCHI
GAESHI
'A'— REPEATS.

* TAI-OTOSHI

* UCHI-MATA

* HARAI
GOSHI

'A' ATTACKS
USING ONE OF
THE ABOVE
THROWS.
'B' AVOIDS.
REPEAT
UNTIL 'B'
IS THROWN.

STING DRILLS

'A' AND 'B'
ATTACK
AND AVOID
UNTIL ONE
IS THROWN

KADORI

AV = AVOID
R = REPEAT

* THESE DRILLS ARE MANDATORY. STUDENTS MUST BE WELL VERSED IN THESE
DRILLS. THE OTHER DRILLS SHOULD BE PRACTICED BUT NOT DWELLED UPON.

DURING THE KADORI STING DRILL EXERCISES THROWS ARE DILIGENTLY
ATTEMPTED. DEFENDERS MAKE NOT THE SLIGHTEST EFFORT TO
PREVENT ATTACKS. DEFENDERS EITHER AVOID AN ATTACK USING AN
AVOIDANCE SKILL OR GET THROWN (THE STING).

THE BULL AND THE MATADOR
STAGE 3 — STEP 4
FIG 26

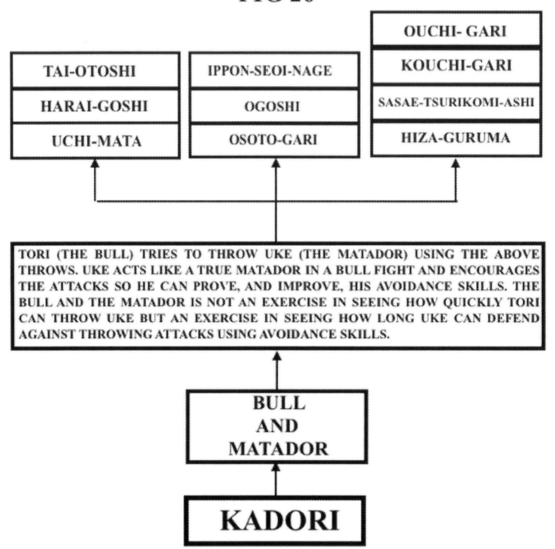

TAI-OTOSHI	IPPON-SEOI-NAGE	OUCHI- GARI
HARAI-GOSHI	OGOSHI	KOUCHI-GARI
UCHI-MATA	OSOTO-GARI	SASAE-TSURIKOMI-ASHI
		HIZA-GURUMA

TORI (THE BULL) TRIES TO THROW UKE (THE MATADOR) USING THE ABOVE THROWS. UKE ACTS LIKE A TRUE MATADOR IN A BULL FIGHT AND ENCOURAGES THE ATTACKS SO HE CAN PROVE, AND IMPROVE, HIS AVOIDANCE SKILLS. THE BULL AND THE MATADOR IS NOT AN EXERCISE IN SEEING HOW QUICKLY TORI CAN THROW UKE BUT AN EXERCISE IN SEEING HOW LONG UKE CAN DEFEND AGAINST THROWING ATTACKS USING AVOIDANCE SKILLS.

BULL AND MATADOR

KADORI

THE BULL AND THE MATADOR IS THE COLLECTIVE PRACTICE OF ALL THE STING DRILLS

FLOATING RANDORI
STAGE 3 STEP 5
FIG 27

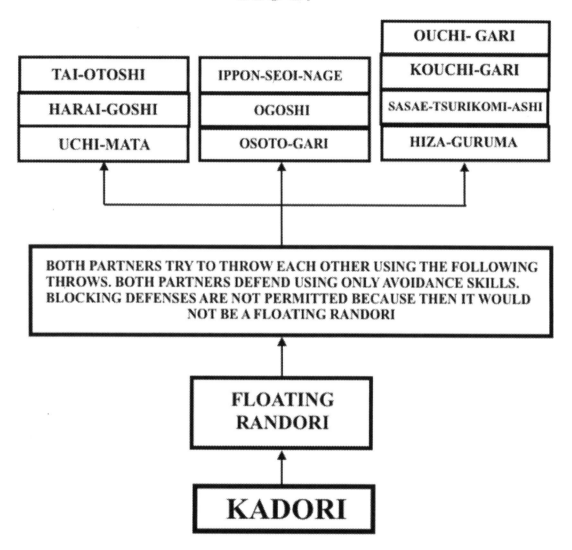

| OUCHI- GARI |
TAI-OTOSHI	IPPON-SEOI-NAGE	KOUCHI-GARI
HARAI-GOSHI	OGOSHI	SASAE-TSURIKOMI-ASHI
UCHI-MATA	OSOTO-GARI	HIZA-GURUMA

BOTH PARTNERS TRY TO THROW EACH OTHER USING THE FOLLOWING THROWS. BOTH PARTNERS DEFEND USING ONLY AVOIDANCE SKILLS. BLOCKING DEFENSES ARE NOT PERMITTED BECAUSE THEN IT WOULD NOT BE A FLOATING RANDORI

FLOATING RANDORI

KADORI

FLOATING RANDORI IS A NATURAL EXTENSION OF
THE BULL AND THE MATADOR

TESTIMONIALS

THE FIVE STEPS
TO RANDORI

Jim Bregman
302 Wildman Street, N. E.
Leesburg, Virginia 20176
10/20/2017
Subject: FIVE STEPS TO RANDORI BY SID KELLY

To whom it may concern,

I would like to whole heartedly recommend that you review, evaluate, and then incorporate into the world wide judo community's curriculum for judo instruction, Mr. Sid Kelly's FIVE STEPS TO RANDORI.

Although I no longer coach/teach judo regularly, I do attend summer training camps and give seminars nation-wide. I have had many opportunities to see the results of this teaching method on the mat and have discussed its benefits with many full-time coaches and club instructors. In the past, I have served multiple terms as a Board Member and President of the United States Judo Association. During that long tenure, one of my greatest concerns was the high drop-out rate for beginners and more senior judo practitioners. Many ideas for the improvement of retention have been widely discussed and tried over the years. Some more successful than others.

I am convinced that the large scale implementation, here, in the United States, and, more broadly, throughout the World Wide Judo Community, of Mr. Kelly's FIVE STEPS TO RANDORI, will improve overall technical quality, understanding of judo principles, enhance retention rates, and make the experience of learning this great art much more enjoyable for many more people. In my opinion and from my personal life experience, I can attest to the fact that the study and practice of judo has many more carry overs into everyday life than just winning medals. It has prepared me for the many challenges and wonderful experiences that a fully lived life can offer.

Your kind consideration of my recommendation would be highly appreciated. Please share your thoughts with me on this matter.

Very Respectfully,
Jim Bregman
Bronze Medalist 1964 Tokyo Olympics and 1965 Sao Paulo World championships
Past President and Board Member of the United States Judo Association
Past Director of Camp Olympus and the Bregman Judo and Karate Club

For all judo instructors, I would like to recommend that you view "Sid Kelly the 5 steps to standing randori" on Youtube.com. Mr. Kelly is a thoughtful judo instructor who has developed a method of teaching which will retain students and enhance their learning experience. I believe it will dramatically improve the student's ability to move into Randori quickly and energetically in a smooth and natural way. Try it!

JIM BREGMAN 10TH DAN. 64 OLYMPIC BRONZE MEDALIST. 65 WORLD BRONZE MEDALIST.

10/14/17
To whom it may concern,

This is a letter of support and testimony as to the effectiveness of Sid Kelly's "The 5 Steps to Randori" process. Sid has created a systematic process of transitioning static judo techniques to applying them in an environment that is conducive to dynamic standing randori, in a simple and safe approach. I believe that this 5-step process could improve the quality and safety of judo clubs throughout the country.

Please consider incorporating Sid's "5 Steps to Randori" process into your judo curriculum, tools, and/or resources.

I was introduced to Sid Kelly's system when my club attended the 2016 New York YMCA Judo Camp. Sid took two of my students (early 20's with 1 year of experience) and taught them "The 5 Steps to Randori" process. Over the next 6 months, it transformed them from typical 'strength and speed' focused fighters to players that other instructors/coaches approached me to comment on how "skillful and technical" their Randori was. Two older Japanese individuals (Kodokan trained) commented that they looked like the competitors "of their generation"… specifically how they "floated to avoid" rather employ a forceful defensive posture.

In my opinion and brief experience, Sid Kelly's System has several elements that could help others:

> It is a systematic, simple, and well-designed process (5 easy steps)
> It is useful for all types of Judo practitioners (competitors, recreational, fitness, 'older' players, etc.)
> It is very useful for school programs where students may practice Judo for a short period of time
> It provides a great transition between practice and shiai (restores the original intention/value of randori)
> It reduces the risk of injury between less-skilled players
> It provides a way for 'older' judoka to practice hard long past their competitive years (Judo loses too many 'older' players as they get injured in randori)

From my experience, I think both beginners and advanced students could benefit from incorporating Sid's "5 Steps to Randori" process into a judo club curriculum, tools, and/or resources. Thank you for your time and consideration!

A little about me:
I have been teaching Judo 4-5 days a week since 1983
I received my 4th degree blackbelt from Ace Sukigara (from the Kodokan in 1950's) and Michi Ishibashi

I have trained many State Champions, National Competitors, World Masters Champions, and one 2008 Beijing Olympic team member
Most of my students are not serious competitors (recreational, physical fitness, self-defense, etc.)

———————————————

Jim Irvine
Global Program Manager–Renault-Nissan Alliance, L&D
Global Program Manager–Nissan Motor Company, Ltd.

NISSAN MOTOR LIMITED & RENAULT-NISSAN ALLIANCE
One Nissan Way, Franklin, TN 37067
Office: +1.615.725.3352

14500 NW HWY 464B
Morriston, Fl.32668

To whom it may concern:

I have been using Sid Kelly's 5 steps to randori with the Gator Judo Club in my capacity as sensei there. The club practices at the University of Florida and primarily consists of undergraduate and graduate students. I have found the five steps to be very useful for a variety of reasons. I am able to introduce newer students to randori-like activities quickly and safety while allowing them to feel and enjoy the flow and movement of judo. I have found that the students introduced to randori this way continue on with the floating, avoidance skills that they learn. It is evident in the way they play judo as they become more experienced. It also encourages my students to attack and to develop confidence in their techniques, rather than becoming frustrated, discouraged and defensive as they do with the traditional method of throwing new students into randori with much more experienced students. In the latter, seemingly every attempt to attack is blocked or abruptly countered. Jigotai and defensive kumi kata soon ensue and the quality of randori as a learning instrument deteriorates.

Students exposed to randori through the five steps go on to be fluid, relaxed and to frequently attempt a variety of throws during randori. The class as a whole learns to distinguish between the different types of randori - "kadori randori, regular randori and shidori randori" in the terminology of the five steps -and is able to play at the level instructed.

Another important benefit is the retention of students, because they are able to experience some of the joy of judo early on while minimizing the frustration of blocked and countered throwing attempts. We have a wide range of students at Gator Judo - some quite athletic and some not so much - but all seem to enjoy the practices and camaraderie of the club. Admittedly I am an advocate of grass roots judo - for which I find the five steps ideal. I do not need or want to winnow out all but the top competitors. For that, the traditional method is fine. Myself, I love to see all kinds of students enjoying active, fluid randori.

Just a note about myself. I started practicing Judo in 1969 when I was a student at Yale University. I have practiced Judo as well as a style of Japanese ju-jitsu during these past 48 years. I hold a Sandan in Judo and a Shichidan in Ju-Jitsu. I have known Sid Kelly for more than half this time and have benefitted greatly from his sage advice and instruction. As long as I have known him, he has wrestled with the problems that beginners encounter during the first months of judo. Problems which include frustration, safety, and developing natural, free-floating and progressive styles of playing judo. Solving these problems in turn solves the major problem of retainment. His "five steps" is the culmination of many years of thought and effort devoted to these issues. I would love to see it applied more widely in the world of Judo.

Sincerely,
Walter Miller

Saturday October 28, 2017

To Whom It May Concern

Re: "Thinking Outside The Judo Box" By Sid Kelly, 8th[th] Dan

I have known Sid Kelly for almost twenty years. During that time I have collaborated with him on a variety of judo related efforts. Sid's background as an engineer is obvious in his writings and presentations. They always follow a logical path. His latest project, "Thinking Outside The Judo Box," is no exception.

I have been fortunate enough to train with Jim Bregman (USA), Ben Campbell (USA), Anton Geesink (Holland) and Geoff Gleeson (UK). Each of these men have influenced me in different ways about judo and it application(s). I first met Sid at a summer camp in New York state (USA). where he was one of the instructors. What I remember and impressed me was that at the end of his session he handed out an outline of what he had covered. With the exception of Mr. G. Gleeson no one else had ever done this to me before.

A few years later I relocated to Connecticut (USA). Being involved locally with Sid gave me an additional appreciation for his approach. About 10 years ago he began discussing and presenting in our dojo what he then called Kelly's Capers. I immediately believed that this approach had great value. Not since my exposure to Mr. G. Gleeson, had someone piqued my interest in a different approach to teaching judo. My own judo really is that of Jim Bregman's (though I never achieved his success). I have coached judoka at the national level, working drill sequences, weight training, tactics, etc., but had not really thought thoroughly about why we lose so many people, so soon. Sid's approach is superficially simple: Describing his approach to seasoned coaches in the USA, their basic response is: "yes, yes, I do that"....the facts are quite different. This cavalier response, I believe, stems from the fact that many coaches are so ingrained with the present system that they believe the present system has all the answers. Even when the present system allows beginners to be introduced to randori when they have none of the necessary skills to apply their learned throws within a non-cooperative environment. At this critical moment of entering judo beginners are left to sort it out for themselves without having any previous training or guidance in the skills needed to apply throws. The judo coaching community can do better than this. In our dojo every new teen/adult begins with Sid's approach. All of our senior students know the system and use it when practicing with new people.

Having been involved in judo since 1961 I find this system to be an excellent tool for any dojo to utilize. My only caution would be for those who have done judo for some time. They will unconsciously do things that sabotage the program, in short, they will need to relearn working with beginners. It's not their fault. It's the systems fault. Today's beginners and practicing judoka were introduced to randori from the aspect of fighting not free-floating judo movements. This is expected to come later with experience. It rarely does. In the meanwhile, large numbers of people drop out of judo because of frustration. Where they can't drop out is in countries where judo is institutionalized, schools, etc. The present system does not bode well for privately run dojos. Because of standing randori frustration, too many students leave well before they find out what fun judo can be once their skills begin to work.

The skills that the 5 steps to randori instills will benefit a judoka well into their judo careers, while allowing them to be better prepared when they enter randori. Better prepared enjoyment wise, safety wise, feelings of skill growth, and the realization that judo can recreational and it's not all about becoming a champion.

Should wish more information from me, please feel free to contact me at:
NorwichJudoDojo@aol.com
USA (860) 917-6318

Respectfully,

Bill Montgomery, 6th Dan

Monday October 30, 2017

To Whom It May Concern,

My name is Bill Myers. I have been the head instructor of Judo at Cornell University in Ithaca, NY since 1994. I have a unique situation in that I teach a beginner class twice a year for 3 months each. During this time, I have my students on the mat for a total of 24 hours. Trying to maximize this time is difficult, but it's amazing what one can accomplish in this seemingly short amount of time.

During these many years, I have taught over 1000 people how to play Judo. My teaching style has changed over the years as well - evolving from the static uchi-komi method by which I was taught, to dynamic throwing and setups, and finally to incorporating Sid Kelly's methods of avoidance and attacking drills. In my experience, Sid's methods are the best way that I've ever seen to get students from zero to competent and confident randori. Using this technique, I was able to get my students to begin randori by the eighth class - and they didn't even know that's what they were doing. To them, it was just an extension of the drills that they were already doing. The focus on uninhibited attacks from the beginning of their judo life will give any judoka a solid foundation for future development. A side note, a co-instructor at Cornell was initially skeptical and thought that his personal teaching methods were superior. However, after observing my classes and doing some personal experimentation, he found that students developed faster when they had something positive to do rather than stiff-arming for defense. He now uses the Five Steps to Randori method.

My personal Judo experience was much different. After learning to break-fall and to do a couple of throws, I was trying to randori in only my second class. But I can tell you that I was completely incompetent and very frustrated with my Judo progress for many years. If I had been taught using the Five Steps to Randori, I would be a much better Judo player today, not having wasted many classes and years figuring things out for myself. Sid's Five Steps to Randori is designed to be incorporated into a regular class and even though it's intended for beginners, I've watched even more advanced Judoka have fun with it. Its effect on my Judo was also significant, even though I've been in Judo for more than 40 years. Its job is simple - get Judoka to feel comfortable attacking and defending in a positive manner. Once this is done, more techniques can be added to their repertoire. I have been to many dojos in the U.S. both in my own study of Judo and during my travels and I have witnessed many poorly run classes with many clueless Judo players. If more dojos used Sid's methods, I believe that the level of Judo would rise significantly, leading to more good players. It makes classes more fun and produces better players. What could be a better combination?

Sincerely,

Bill Myers 4th Dan Judo Cornell University Judo Club

To Whom it May Concern

Like many of you out there, I have attended many seminars by numerous advanced students, competitors and coaches. Over the years, many of these lectures became a giant melting pot of the same techniques taught the same way. Kelly's Capers changed all that. Why? How? Because Kelly's Capers is judo! Jigoro Kano said it first and best, "maximum efficiency, minimum effort." Kelly's Capers does this by improving posture, timing, and fluid movement in randori, and is a completely new approach to teaching the world's greatest art. Along with 33 other coaches I attended the 2010 USJA/USJF Winter Nationals Coach Certification Clinic. Honestly, I was hoping to pick up a nugget or two of worthwhile ideas or techniques to incorporate into my own lesson plans. However, I have now implemented the entire Capers program into my daily workouts at our dojo. From one coach to the entire judo community, Kelly's Capers is a worthwhile endeavor! This program creates a bridge for new and experienced players alike to hone their randori skills in a practice format that is dynamic rather than stagnant. As a coach I highly recommend judoka everywhere to find a clinic on Kelly's Capers and participate.

Pastor/Sensei Bob Rush

To Whom it May Concern,

Kelly's Capers is a phenomenal system of teaching judo. Even though it is marketed towards beginners, it really is something that helps all levels. There were a couple of seasoned masters at the clinic who said they would be practicing it themselves because they felt it would give them more of an edge in competition. Everyone I spoke to about Kelly's Capers loved it, from orange belt teenagers, to competitors, to coaches. Sid, congratulations for literally revolutionizing the way we think about teaching judo.

Chris Maurer
Ridgewood Judo.

KATA

(FORM PRACTICE)

JUDO FOR EVERYONE
THE KATA CHART - FIG 28

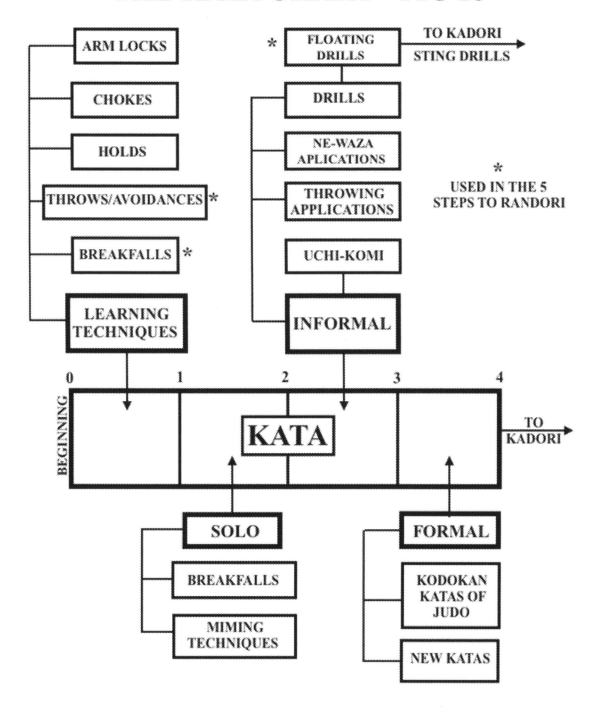

KATA
(FORM PRACTICE)

The judo practice of form, which is to inform
Is for many, the norm.
But practicing formal form, also to inform,
Is for very many, not the norm.
AND
Kata, the Japanese word for form,
Elicits opinions that are far from uniform.
Some believe kata is the final word,
While others think it's madness, or absurd.

Kata - the study of form - separate from the study of applying skills, is shown on page 77 - Fig 28. Every future action, except intuitive actions derived from competitiveness, will first be formed from a person's study of kata.

From the Kata Chart it can be seen Kata is divided into four sections. Kata is not known to have a hierarchical Classification — kata is just known as kata. But the following four sections shows there is some necessary order of application.

1) Learning Techniques
2) Solo Form Exercises
3) Informal Form Exercises
4) Formal Form Exercises

1) LEARNING TECHNIQUES
This section is where it all starts for everyone and this learning is not a one-time affair. As progress is made and new techniques are taught this learning section is returned to again and again. It is here the basic techniques of break-falling, throwing, holding, choking, arm-locking, and defending against techniques are introduced.

2) SOLO FORM EXERCISES.
After learning some basic techniques, and whatever is learned later, Solo Form Exercises are the easiest of the kata practices. Solo practice of break-falls is a life-long practice and so can be miming whatever judo movement has been learned

3) INFORMAL FORM EXERCISES.

Informal Form Exercises differ from Formal Form Exercises in that they are not concerned with practicing movements with respect to a specific direction — towards a seat of honor (Joseki). Informal Form, contrary to solo practice, practices with a partner, one applying a technique (tori) while the other is receiving it (uke). The Informal form uses learned basic techniques applied in many ways. These include:

1) Uchikomi — repetitions of a single technique.
2) Ukemi with a partner.
3) Throw for Throw.
4) Drills — repeating a series of actions:
   a) Combining throws
   b) Countering throws.
   c) Transitioning from throwing to newaza.
   d) Transitioning grappling techniques in all their multitudinous forms.

4) FORMAL FORM EXERCISES.

Formal Form consists of eight Kodokan katas. These are practiced in the dojo as a recreational pastime or in a kata competition where partners compete against other partners. This is the only time there is competitiveness in kata. The eight Kodokan katas are:

1) Nage-no-Kata (Forms of Throwing).
2) Katame-no-Kata (Forms of Grappling or Holding).
3) Kime-no-Kata (Forms of Decisive Techniques).
4) Ju-no-Kata (Forms of Gentleness and Flexibility).
5) Kodokan Goshi Jutsu ((Forms of Kodokan Self Defense).
6) Itsutsu-no-kata (Forms of Five).
7) Koshiki-noKata (Forms of Classics).
8) Seiryoku-Zenyo-Kokumin-Taiiku (Forms of Maximum-Efficiency National physical education).

JUDO FOR EVERYONE
THE FIRST TWO STEPS TO RANDORI
FIG 29

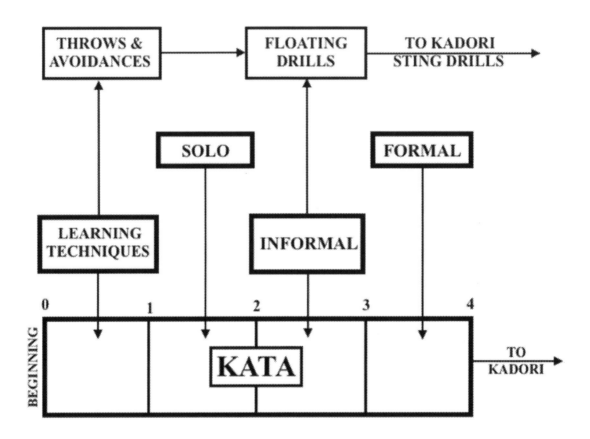

FLOATING DRILLS — STEP 2 OF THE 5 STEPS

Floating Drills are repetitive exercises that combine throws with avoidance defenses. Floating Drills are somewhat like the throwing exercise Throw for Throw except instead of taking a breakfall after being thrown, uke rides or avoids the throw. H/ she is then attacked again with the same throw and the same exercise is repeated again by uke avoiding the throw. Floating drills are really preparation drills for Sting Drills. A Floating Drill is a kata repetition exercise of going through the motions of attacking with the same throw and avoiding the attack with the same avoidance movement. A Sting Drills is the repetition exercise of a Floating Drill, except tori is really trying to throw uke. It is a kadori exercise. It is a competitive Floating drill. The better students are at Floating Drills the easier it will be for them to adapt to the next three steps — Sting Drills, the Bull and the Matador and Floating Randori.

The names Floating Drills and Sting Drills are named after the great heavyweight boxing champion Mohammed Ali's, world-famous quote, 'Float like a Butterfly and Sting Like Bee.' The floating refers to his floating style of boxing and the sting refers to his punch when he knocked them out. Floating drills refer to judo drills where the defender rides or avoids throwing attacks with free floating avoidance moves (kata). Sting drills are floating drills applied competitively (kadori) and the sting occurs when a throw is made.

AVOIDING THROWS

Avoidance skills are central to the five steps to randori. It is by using only avoidance skills (no stiff arming and hip blocking) that randori skills, not competitive skills, can more quickly be learned. Avoiding being thrown using only body movements is the purest of judo defenses. But it is not the most effective. Nothing is more effective than a pair of stiff arms nullifying a throw before it even begins. That's why so many people stiff arm their way through their judo life. They want to play it safe. But playing it safe leaves them exactly where they were before the throw being blocked started — their skill development remained at zero. And take this zero and multiply it by hundreds or thousands and you still get zero. On the other hand, by taking risks, by allowing attacks to happen and using only avoidance defenses (kadori) judo skills, that is, free bodily floating movements, timing, distant judgement, sense of feel, mind body co-ordination, and anticipation will grow exponentially. After a thorough grounding in such practice, hip and arm blocking defenses can easily be added at a later date. The martial can easily be added to the art, but the art cannot be so easily added to the martial. Mats are full of people trying to undue bad practice habits which were early formed through no fault of their own or their instructors. It was the result of the system — a system that did not prepare them with the skills needed to apply and defend against throwing attacks. They learned to defend against throwing attacks through osmosis — stiff arming. But stiff arming in randori is detrimental to skill development.

THROWING AVOIDANCES DESCRIBED

The five steps to randori uses ten throws and their avoidance defenses. The throws and avoidances are introduced gradually through three stages. The ten avoidances along with some guidelines are described below:

GUIDELINES

1) Because the action of each throw is different each avoidance is obviously different. But the avoidance principle is always the same. The defender always harmonizes, blends or follows the path of the forces of the thrower's action.

2) The more a defender remains relaxed the more effective his avoidances will be.

3) All descriptions are for right side attacks.

4) Clockwise and counter-clockwise descriptions are viewed from above.

5) Descriptions describe defensive and the off balancing follow up actions only. Throwing actions following off balancing are not described because each situation is or could be different.

6) Throws are grouped into the three stages of the five steps to randori.

STAGE 1

The avoidance defenses for Stage 1 can be found on YouTube — Judo Sid Kelly 5 steps to randori. But for sake of completeness the avoidances are described below.

1) **Major Outer Reaping (Osoto-gari)**
   (A) attacks (B) with Osoto-gari. With (A) positioned fully forward on his left foot without his reaping right leg yet engaged, (B) turns 90 degrees clockwise and walks forward off balancing (A).

2) **Major Hip Throw (Ogoshi)**
   (A) attacks (B) with Ogoshi. Just before (A's) back contacts (B's) front, (B) moves 180 degrees counter-clockwise around in front of (A) and walks forward and off balances (A).

3) **One Armed Shoulder Throw (Ippon Seoi-nage)**
   (A) attacks (B) with Ippon-seoi-nage. During the latter part of the throwing entry, just before (A's) back contacts (B's) front, (B) rides the throw with his left forearm bracing (not pushing) against (A's) back. Landing on the mat in front of (A), (B) walks forward and off balances (A).

STAGE 2

4) **Major Inner Reaping Throw (Ouchi-gari)**
   (A) attacks (B) with Ouchi-gari. With his left leg completely relaxed (B) allows his leg to be lifted by (A's) reaping action and places the sole of his left

foot on (A's) left Achilles heel in preparation for a right Ni-dan-kosoto-gari throw.

5) **Minor Inner Reaping Throw (Kouchi-gari)**
(A) attacks (B) with Kouchi-gari. With his right leg completely relaxed (B) allows his leg to be lifted by (A's) reaping action and places the sole of his right foot on outside of (A's) left knee in preparation for a left hiza guruma throw.

6) **Propping Drawing Ankle Throw (Sasae-tsuri-komi-ashi)**
(A) attacks (B) with Sasae-tsurikomi-ashi. Anticipating (A's) left foot propping the front of his right ankle (B) lifts his right foot up and pivots counterclockwise on his left foot. On returning his right foot to the mat he continues moving counterclockwise around (A) while hopping on his right foot and places the sole of his left foot on the outside of (A's) right knee in preparation for a right Hiza-guruma throw.

7) **Knee wheel Throw (Hiza-guruma)**
(A) attacks (B) with Hiza-guruma. As (A) steps in a counterclockwise direction on to his right foot (B) follows (A's) path of movement by stepping towards (A) with his left foot. (B) literally walks in-between (A's) legs and off balances him backwards.

STAGE 3
8) **Body Drop Throw (Tia-otoshi)**
(A) attacks (B) with Tia-otoshi. Avoiding (A's) attacking outstretched right leg (B) lifts his right leg up and jumps over and in front of (A) and moves around in a counterclockwise direction. Continuing to move counterclockwise around (A). (B) places his left sole on the outside of (A's) right knee in preparation for a right Hiza-guruma throw.

9) **Sweeping Loin Throw (Harai-goshi)**
(A) attacks (B) with Harai-goshi.
   a) With (A) standing on his driving left leg, just prior to sweeping his right leg, (B) side steps to his left with his left foot and unbalances (A).
   b) As (A) is turning and nearly completed his entry (B) steps forward and unbalances (A).

10) **Inner Thigh Throw (Uchi-mata)**
(A) attacks (B) with Uchi-mata.
   a) With (A) standing on his driving left leg, just prior to sweeping his right leg, (B) side steps to his left with his left foot and unbalances (A).
   b) As (A) is turning and nearly completed his entry (B) steps forward and unbalances (A).

83

KADORI

(RANDORI PREPARATION)

WHY THE NEED FOR KADORI

The old English proverb, 'Necessity is the mother of invention — the primary driving force for most new inventions, is a need. In judo there is a need. There's been a need ever since competitive judo (shiai) was introduced to Kodokan judo. Dr Kano critically noted, "competitive judo changed the way randori was practiced. He said, 'in randori there is now an increase in the strength verses strength or wrestling type practice.' (see Judo Memoirs of Jigoro Kano, by Brian N. Watson).

Because strength verses strength, wrestling type randori, has been practiced for six judo generations, it is, for most instructors and practitioners, the judo norm. Of course, those that stay the course and iron out the randori bugs, can be seen applying judo skills with dexterity. But with the high turnover rate the mat is witness to strength versus strength wrestling type practice. What the public sees turns them off. So there is a need! A need for something that will attract more people to try judo and stay in judo.

Instructors are not to blame for judo's lack of popularity. They are as frustrated as anybody else. They are doing the best they can with the methods of training they inherited — kata - randori - shiai. But therein lies the problem. The direct kata to randori transition leads to strength verses strength wrestling type practice (to again quote Dr. Kano). This transition does not take into account that students completely lack even the most fundamental skills to practice standing randori. So, students compensate and muscle it out by practicing a going nowhere randori. The harder they try (and many do try so hard), the more it turns into a judo fight (contest). The harder they contest the worse it seems to get (no results). Then they end up frustrated and leave. The traditional expectation is you can only acquire randori skills by lots and lots of randori — practice practice practice and all will be revealed. Which, when you are into and acclimated to randori, is true. But getting into and acclimating to randori requires time and fortitude. And because the 21st century is not known for producing too many samurai warriors from civilians, judo classes will remain small.

What is needed is a method that will gradually introduce students to the skills required for randori. This needs to be done while the student is still in a comfort zone of agreeing with h/her partner what they are going to do (kata), while at the same time practicing in a competitive environment (randori) where they are able try out the basic throwing techniques they know.

This method is Kadori — see The Kadori Chart - Page 88 - Fig 30.

THE KADORI CHART
(RANDORI PREPARATION)
FIG 30

STEPS 3 - 4 - 5
OF
THE 5 STEPS TO RANDORI

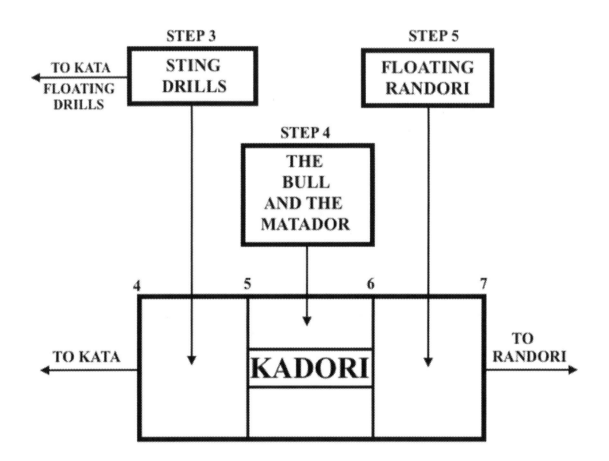

KADORI
(RANDORI PREPARATION)

Kadori is the new kid on the block,
Which is a practice with a lot of sock.
Randori competitiveness is gradually introduced,
While skills are unknowingly produced.

It begins in kata with no frills,
With the practice of floating drills.
Floating drills then change to Sting drills in kadori,
Giving skill development a different story.

Sting drills then progress to the Bull and Matador,
Where the matador is frequently on the floor.
The bull is allowed to give it his all,
While the matador learns from every fall.

The next kadori exercise is Floating Randori,
Exposing a new practice in all its glory.
Where both can attack and defend uninhibited.
Because the rules for defending are restricted.

Kadori is the missing category between kata and randori — coined from the words KAta and ranDORI. Kadori is a mixture of kata and randori. It is the bridge between kata and randori. It does not and cannot replace kata or randori because it is neither one nor the other. When practicing kadori both partners follow a strictly agreed pattern of events — kata — but with some competitiveness — randori. Kadori has three functions or uses derived from kata and randori. First. Form can be practiced in a competitive environment (randori) without the attacker being blocked from trying (kata). Second. Partners agree on exactly what moves they are going to practice beforehand and do not deviate from them (kata). Third. It is a competitive skill building exercise (randori). Although kadori can be used in preparing some judo grappling skills the reference here is to standing randori only.

The function of the new category (kadori) is to rectify the present competitive disconnect between kata and randori. To understand this the functions of kata and randori have to be fully appreciated. First, kata. When two people are engaged in any practice to improve their martial art form there is a mutual agreement that whatever they are practicing will not be deviated from and there will be no resistance to the actions of whatever is being practiced. Second, randori. When two people are engaged in free practice THERE is a shared agreement, WHETHER they know it or not, THAT the practice is about us, not about me. Randori is not about (me) winning, but about (us) improving. In a contest it's about (me) winning and (you) losing. Randori practice has to be competitive, for without resistance there can be no realistic evaluation of a particular martial skill. So kadori functions as both some kata and some randori which ends up being a practical way of removing the contesting tendencies that usually occur when beginners are immersed cold turkey into randori.

THE ADVANTAGES OF KADORI EXERCISES

1) A specific skill can be isolated and focused upon in a combined kata/randori (cooperative/noncooperative) environment.
2) After isolation, practitioners are able to attempt a skill many times in a limited competitive environment.
3) Randori competitiveness is introduced very gradually.
4) Compared with randori, a specific skill can be developed exponentially because a specific competitive action can be experienced many times during a short period.
5) In randori the opportunity to try a new skill may rarely occur. When it does occur the experience needed to seize the opportunity is usually initially lacking. But with kadori repetition, opportunities are far more frequent and skills have a far greater chance of developing.

As shown on the kadori chart Fig 30 page 88, Kadori is divided into the following three exercises:

1) STING DRILLS
2) THE BULL AND THE MATADOR
3) FLOATING RANDORI

STING DRILLS

A Sting Drill is an extension of a kata Floating Drill (see page 81). The difference being the intent of tori is to throw uke not demonstrate with him. The tempo is competitive, but because both partners know what's coming next (kata), the outcome is determined by the effectiveness of the speed and power of the throw (randori), or the slowness or mistiming of the avoidance skill (randori). This is the first introduction to competitiveness but because it is so slight it is very easy for both partners to adjust to. Below is an example of a Sting Drill.

THE OSOTO-GARI STING DRILL

After some maneuvering tori enters with the intention of throwing uke with Osoto-gari. Uke puts up absolutely no resistance to the Osoto-gari attack but avoids being thrown using an avoidance skill (floats like a butterfly) or takes a fall (stings like a bee). The sequence of a Sting Drill is as follows. First. Tori attacks on the right and uke defends. This is done for a decided period of time or until uke is thrown. Second. They change roles. Third. They change partners. Fourth. This whole procedure is repeated on the left side. When both are well versed with left and right side attacking they now proceed as follows. Tori now attacks on either the left or right side. Tori may attack as before, directly to the right or left, or he may feint to one side before attacking on the other. From this early exercise practitioners are introduced to the competitive skills of breaking balance by feinting from left to right or right to left. And this is before they've even started to randori.

THE BULL AND THE MATADOR

The Bull and the Matador is as the title suggests. One person, the bull, continually attacks and tries to throw (toss) the matador. The matador skillfully avoids the attacks or gets tossed (takes a fall). As in a bullfight, the bull is free to attack because the matador is moving around waiting to be attacked. And when attacked h/she rides or avoids the throw, but never blocks an attack. Otherwise, it wouldn't be a Bull and Matador replica. The bull now attacks (using all three throws - Stage 1 of the 5 steps — or ten throws on reaching Stage 3. Like a true matador h/she allows the attacks to happen and even encourages them. From this exercise the habit of uninhibited attacking is formed and avoidance skills are severely tested.

FLOATING RANDORI

In this final kadori exercise the mode of application takes a big change. In the Floating Drills, Sting Drills and the Bull and the Matador the mode of application was that one attacked and the other defended. And each drill built on the other by more throws being added along the way. Floating Randori is different. Here both partners attack and defend

Floating Randori is the quintessential method of developing the art of throwing avoidance skills. By defending using only avoidance techniques against throwing attacks the strength aspect of physically preventing throwing attacks has been removed. Strength is now limited to the efforts of trying and applying throws. Floating Randori is an ideal exercise for preparing beginners for regular randori and a refreshing exercise in practicing pure judo (floating practice) for experienced players.

RANDORI
(FREE PRACTICE)

SKILL DEVELOPMENT

RANDORI FOR EVERYONE
THE RANDORI CHART
FIG 31

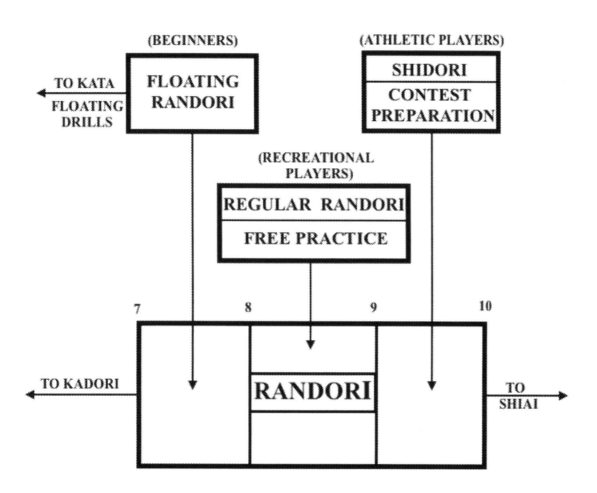

RANDORI
(FREE PRACTICE)

Free practice, known as randori,
Gives every judo skill a story.
Freedom of flow in body and mind,
Is the elusive ideal to find.
AND
The years gradually pass with randori the measure,
Loosing, speed, timing, endurance, and all you treasure.
So it's back down to the mat where you're able,
To holds, chokes, and arm locks, and all things stable.

Then, when your choked and groping for a trick,
And no longer quick, nothing seems to click.
Finally, when all is spent and you've had your fill,
You realize once and for all your over the hill.

RANDORI — AS A METHOD OF PRACTICE
Randori is doing the best you can with the skills you have in order to make them better than they were before.

Randori - known as free practice - is the exercise that develops skills to competitively apply the techniques learned in kata. Although randori includes developing both throwing and grappling skills this analysis only covers throwing. Because so many people find learning and applying throwing skills elusive, and drop out prematurely, this study has created three methods of randori. This will cater for three distinct groups of students: beginners, recreational, and athletic players — see the randori chart, page 95 - Fig 31.

But wether it be one or three methods of randori, randori is the most effective method of developing skills needed to execute throws in a competitive environment: some of these are: breaking balance (kuzushi), blending or fitting actions (tsukuri), the throwing action or execution (kake), consisting of the appreciation and coordinated use of — the locking arm, the power arm, the driving leg, the active leg, and the angle of attack, — agility, flexibility, maximizing speed and acceleration, synchronous timing, muscular co-ordination (muscle memory), consistent exactness of movement, harmony, reaction, explosiveness, distance judgement, the correct use of power, gripping, a medium posture adaptable to attacking and defending, consistent balanced walking, efficient leveraging, maneuvering, following through, the defensive skills of avoidance, blocking, and twisting out, and the falling ways in all their multitudinous forms.

Simultaneously, developing and evolving with the above listed physical skills, are by-products that are subliminally, and subconsciously produced. Some of these are: physical and mental coordination, persistence, decisiveness, discipline, fighting spirit, determination, concentration, patience, alertness, physical fitness, stamina, endurance, instinctive realization of throwing opportunities, determining the difference between realistic and unrealistic knowledge, and pain tolerance.

Listed below are ten elementary skills, with some explanations, that develop with the regular practice of randori.

INTANGIBLE RANDORI SKILLS (CAN'T BE LEARNED BY KATA)
1) Maneuvering:
   Subconsciously correctly positioning the body in order to apply or defend throwing attacks through correct walking.

2) Balanced Walking:
   Linked with maneuvering, balanced walking between attacking and defending actions.

3) A Sense of Feel;
   Hand and brain co-ordination. From this co-ordination a sense of knowing is developed of when to attack and defend. This sense of feel can never be cultivated with stiffness and rigidity.

4) Responsive Gripping:
   Releasing and retaking a grip, adjusting a grip, immediately attacking after changing a grip, and defending while gripping are all skills acquired from hands on experience. (excuse the pun).

5) Synchronized Timing:
   Timing that is synchronized with the opponents maneuvering, attacking and defending movements (related to synchronized harmony).

6) Adjusting to or Creating Tempo:
   Creating a tempo and acting, accepting a tempo and acting, or re-creating a tempo and acting.

7) Synchronized Harmony:
   Harmonizing with the opponent's movements when maneuvering, attacking and defending (related to synchronized timing).

8) **Physical and Mental Co-ordination:**
   Mind and body working in unison when maneuvering, attacking and defending.

9) **Spacial Awareness:**
   The instinctive awareness of the correct distance needed between two bodies during maneuvering, attacking and defending.

10) **Free Floating Movements:**
    It is only with free floating relaxed movements that the above activities can be effectively applied. If this is true, then having free floating relaxed movements is the most important element or component in standing randori (let the reader be the judge).

THROWING RANDORI ENTITIES

Alphabetically listed are thirty-five entities (skills, qualities, elements), that either occur, or influence results, during throwing practice (randori).

1) A sense of feel.
2) A sense of knowing, of how and when to apply an action.
3) Accuracy of movement.
4) Alternating muscle relaxation and tensioning.
5) Avoiding a throw by round offs and turn outs.
6) Avoiding a throw using body movement (tai-sabaki).
7) Balance.
8) Blocking a throw using the hand(s) and arm(s).
9) Blocking a throw using the hips.
10) Break-falling.
11) Control.
12) Correct breathing.
13) Correct reactions
14) Counter throwing.
15) Distance judgement.
16) Enjoyment (or the lack of– a by-product of the other 34entities).
17) Experience.
18) Explosiveness.
19) Fighting spirit.
20) Grip fighting.
21) Gripping (optimum).
22) Harmony.
23) Judo power.
24) Mental-physical coordination.
25) Physical fitness (randori fitness).
26) Positive attitude.
27) Posture.
28) Speed.
29) Tactical maneuvering.
30) Tempo.
31) Throwing (entry-balance breaking-throwing action).
32) Timing.
33) Tussling (vigorous struggling)
34) Unpredictability of opponent.
35) Walking.

The development of the above entities is more a result of the wonders of the human mind body connection than randori practice. Regular practice of tennis would produce a different timing skill — that of hitting a fast-moving ball bouncing at a compound angle.

THE
THREE TYPES
OF
RANDORI

RANDORI CHOICES

From the Randori chart Page 95 - Fig 31 it can be seen there are three methods of randori. These three methods develop different skills at different levels of competitiveness. With these three choices a practitioner can now select a practice h/she wishes to focus on. H/she can use the lighter practices (Floating and Regular Randori) to warm up before practicing Contest Randori (Shidori), or if h/she is not in a competitive mood, h/she can bypass practicing the more competitive practice of shidori and just practice Floating Randori or Regular Randori. H/she now has choices. Whereas, with the present one choice of randori h/she would have to fit into the mood or desires of h/her partner which may or may not be to h/her liking.

1)   FLOATING RANDORI

From Page 88 - Fig 30 it can be seen that Floating Randori is the last of the kadori exercises, and the last of the five steps to randori. It is also the first of the randori exercises. Although titled the same, the kadori Floating Randori and randori Floating Randori represent two different situations. The kadori Floating Randori Page 88 - Fig 30 is when Floating Randori is first learned. The Floating Randori of Page 95 - Fig 31 is when Floating Randori it is known and being practiced. It should also be noted that the regular practice of Floating Randori is connected to Beginner's Contesting because their actions are fundamentally the same. See Beginner's Contest Chart Page 119 - Fig 33.

Although Floating Randori is the first of the three randori exercises it is still technically a kadori exercise (kadori-randori). This is because it is governed by a restriction; defending against throwing attacks only with tai-sabaki avoidances. Floating Randori is the quintessential kadori exercise because it is the sum total of many kadori drills. When first practiced by beginners in preparation for regular randori Floating Randori consists of randomly practicing the Osoto-gari, Ogoshi, and Ippon-seoi-nage kadori drills. But later, seven more throws with their kadori drills are added and practiced. Like the previous kadori drills, Floating Randori practice is a mixture of kata and randori and it is this mix of kata essence and randori essence that governs how Floating Randori is practiced.

THE KATA ESSENCE
1) When defending against a throw only tai-sabaki avoidance movements are allowed.
2) Both partners are openly exposed to being attacked. (no premeditated defending).
3) Both partners become aware that it's a mutual practice (it's about us - not me).

THE RANDORI ESSENCE
1) Both are trying to throw each other.
2) Both are trying not to be thrown.

Because of the kata randori mix in Floating Randori there is an absence of stiff arming. This makes it more practical, safer and enjoyable for beginners to develop their newly learned throws. Floating Randori does not and is not intended to develop fighting skills. This comes later with the severer practice of Contest Randori (shidori) and to some extent Regular Randori. At first this may seem contrary to how most people understand and practice randori; and it is. This is because it's not randori in the traditional sense. Floating Randori is an exercise that prepares students for the skills they will need for standing randori. It is an exercise that was developed for beginners because there is presently no exercise that prepares beginners for standing randori. Knowing how to do some throws and being able to break-fall is not being prepared for randori. Floating Randori is the epitome of pure standing judo.

When Floating Randori is practiced correctly there is no strength involved. There is no constant or intermittent effort being used to prevent the other person from attacking. The only effort being used is in attempting throws, throwing, and in the floating avoidances. This results in a lot of action and the development of many skills. When beginners practice Floating randori the results can sometimes be amazing. Whereas, many experienced players who have established ingrained fighting styles paradoxically have a lot of trouble with free floating avoidances. Many skills are experienced (not mastered) in a shorter period of time using Floating Randori than with Regular Randori or Contest Randori (shidori). This is because the prevention factor (constant or intermittent arm blocking of attacks) is not present.

SUMMARY
FLOATING RANDORI is the first of the three randori exercises and was derived from the Kadori exercises of:

1) Learning throws and their avoidances.
2) Floating Drills.
3) Sting Drills.
4) The Bull and the Matador.
5) Floating Randori.

FLOATING RANDORI is the purest of the randori practices because the use of blocking with the hands and the arms is obsoleted by having only one method of defense: Tai-sabaki avoidances.

REGULAR RANDORI — PRE-AMBLE
As noted on page 9, randori is positioned between kata and shiai. Both kata and shiai have clear cut guidelines or borders to work within. Whereas randori does not. The kata guideline is — no resistance while learning form. The contest guideline is — competitive resistance while trying to win a judo contest. The only guideline

the present one type of randori has is human judgement, which means what is light for one is heavy for another, and what is exhausting for one is just warming up for another. Which means many people are practicing at a level of difficulty they are not enjoying. Because of the lack of randori guidelines three methods of randori have evolved: Floating Randori for beginners, Contest Randori for the athletically inclined (the randori presently most practiced) and again in the middle, Regular Randori.

2) REGULAR RANDORI

Regular Randori is more challenging than Floating Randori. Regular Randori has two ways a to prevent a throw from happening, instead of one as Floating Randori has. Regular Randori can defend against a throw by either avoidance moves or reaction hip blocking. By limiting defending against throwing attacks with only these two methods it means the hands and arms have no part in stopping a throw. The hands are only used to grip the uniform, not prevent attacks. This leads to a very lively unrestricted practice. When both students agree to practice Regular Randori their practice can be very enjoyable and educational. When Regular Randori is practiced correctly there is plenty of enjoyable learning, attacks can easily be attempted because attacks are not prevented from happening. But the objective of the attacks — throws — are prevented from happening by only two methods — avoidances and hip blocking.

SUMMARY

Regular Randori, like its forerunner Floating Randori, is a bilateral (about us) skill development exercise. It is not a unilateral (about me) contest exercise. The various levels of randori difficulty are gaged by how throwing attacks are defended against, not by the severity of the attacks themselves. That is why Contest Randori is the most difficult — constant hand - arm blocking. Whereas Floating Randori is much easier — using only avoidance defenses. Building on the experience gained from practicing Floating Randori (defending with body avoidances), Regular Randori adds reaction hip blocking as a defense. The offshoot of this is Regular Randori produces a practice that is competitive, rigorous, educational, free floating, and playful that has the two following defensive guidelines:

1) Tai - sabaki avoidances.
2) Reactive hip blocking.

CONTEST RANDORI — PREAMBLE

As previously mentioned, when having only one choice of randori the boundaries for determining randori intensity are based on human judgement. The practitioners themselves have to mutually agree upon determining the intensity of the practice. And as humans have quite a reputation for disagreeing on so many things it is inevitable that people of unlike minds and attitudes will often not harmonize during a randori practice. This is often a problem for beginners and experienced recreational players. When they're practicing with someone who wants to go all-out they usually won't say they don't wish to practice so intensely. Because of ego or pride they continue practicing Contest Randori week after week, month after month, until they have had enough and just stop turning up for classes. Hence the need for three methods of randori. Of course, there is absolutely nothing wrong with hard randori practice. It's what devoted judo players relish. However, it is better that only people of like minds practice hard together, and the avenue for this togetherness is Contest Randori (Shidori).

3)   CONTEST RANDORI (SHIDORI)

Contest Randori is a no-holds-barred randori (within the contest rules). This is where a person can either go all out just for his own satisfaction, or in preparing for a contest. It is the exercise where learned skills are honed under contest conditions. It is the most difficult of the three methods of randori practice but the one with the easiest guidelines to follow (both agree the physical activity will be like that of a contest). Because Contest Randori guidelines are so easy to follow the majority of present day Regular Randori now tends to be oriented towards Contest Randori. With the choice of three methods of randori, beginners, recreational and competitive players can now agree upon which method of randori they wish to practice. This is a tremendous clarifying help for both instructors and students. Contest Randori is the most competitive of the three methods of randori and uses the following methods of defending:

1)   Tai-sabaki avoidances
2)   Reactive arm blocking
3)   Reactive hip blocking
4)   Defensive arm blocking
     (within IJF Contest Rules)
5)   Defensive stances
     (within IJF Contest Rules)
6)   Grip fighting
     (within IJF Contest Rules)
7)   Somersaulting to avoid a score.
     (within IJF Contest Rules)

JUDO FOR EVERYONE

SUMMATION OF RANDORI TYPES

1) **FLOATING RANDORI (Kadori Randori)**
    Uses the Defending Methods of:
    a) Tai-sabaki avoidances

    FOR INFO ON THE KADORI 5 STEPS -
    See YouTube — judo Sid Kelly the 5 steps to randori
    skelly111@frontier.com (address subject as — 5 steps)

2) **REGULAR RANDORI (Free Practice)**
    Uses the Defending Methods of:
    a) Tai-sabaki avoidances
    b) Reactive hip blocking

3) **CONTEST RANDORI (Shidori)**
    Uses the Defending Methods of:
    a) Tai-sabaki avoidances
    b) Reactive arm blocking
    c) Reactive hip blocking
    d) Defensive arm blocking
    (within IJF Contest Rules)
    e) Defensive stances
    (within IJF Contest Rules)
    f) Grip fighting
    (within IJF Contest Rules)
    g) Somersaulting to avoid a score.
    (within IJF Contest Rules)

SHIAI

(CONTEST)

JUDO FOR EVERYONE
THE SHIAI CHART
FIG 32

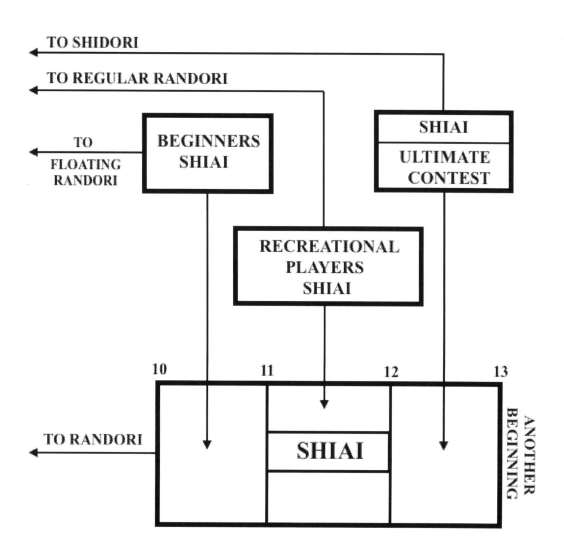

SHIAI
(CONTEST)
JUDO'S ULTIMATE TEST

The paths of judo are varied and diverse,
But success demands you must immerse.
All roads lead to the ultimate goal,
Of making one's judo complete and whole.

Shiai, the Japanese word for contest,
Is the judo players ultimate test,
As all experiences come to the fore,
When executing the decisive score.

SHIAI — CONTEST
(Shiai is doing the the best you can with the skills you have in order to win).

The present contest system tries to fairly match partners of equal experience. Whatever size or however important an event may be, lower and higher grades are always separated. There may be divisions for 6th kyu to 4th kyu — 3rd kyu to 1st kyu — 1st dan and above. If there is a shortage of competitors then the range of experience could be quite broad, such as: 6th kyu to 2nd kyu — 1st kyu and above. But whatever the ranges are and whatever the event is, the type of contest is always the same — the one inherited with the founding of judo, which now has a different set of rules that have evolved over time. To reach and satisfy a broader audience than just the athletically inclined, it is suggested that two new preparatory types of contest be created. These are dojo contests that prepare for the public Ultimate Contest. From the Shiai Chart Page 111 - Fig 32, these new preparatory shiai along with the traditional shiai are shown. Their page references are as below:

1) Beginner's Contest (new)
   (see page 119).

2) Recreational Contest (new)
   (see page 125).

3) Ultimate Contest. (Identical to present contests under IJF rules).
   (see page 129).

Shiai is a judo players greatest test. By definition, a judo contest is a judo match between two contestants with the outcome of one being declared the winner, and the other, by default, the loser.

In one's early days of contesting, a contest seems to be no more than a very hard randori practice with a consequence of either being the winner or the loser. But as time goes by and one begins to take contesting seriously, it begins to take on a completely different meaning. First, you incessantly try and improve your judo skills with randori, which is an elusive and evasive undertaking, to say the least. Then you become aware that without being fit, the time between your entry and exit salutations is going to be very short. Then you realize that it would be very advantageous for you to be not only fit, but very fit, or even super fit. Therefore, besides the many hours spent training on the mat, many hours are spent on supplementary exercises such as running and weight training.

Then comes the day that a competitor experiences complete confidence in being able to score with a specific technique. This realization usually occurs after being successful with a particular technique in a contest. Sometimes it may not be the technique h/she has spent a lot of time on. It just happens to be the one his mind and body coordinate with best. It's just the one, or perhaps two or three that works for h/her under the conditions of duress.

After gaining more years of experience many factors come into play; the psychological aspects of contesting — appearing confident and not being fazed by the importance of an event, grip fighting within the rules, strategies and tactics, being knowledgeable on the rules (or should be), the needed fighting spirit and determination, and enjoying the wins and cheerfully learning from the losses.

Therefore, every time a judo contestant steps on the mat to compete, everything about his judo and him/herself is about to be tested. Besides all the work that h/she has done to prepare him/herself for the contest, h/she carries with h/her all that has affected h/her judo up to that moment; all h/her past contests, h/her past coaching, h/her earlier teachers, what and how h/she was taught, all the different partners h/she has practiced with, all the different dojos h/she has visited, and h/her personal life, including h/her family and h/her work. After ha-jime is given, the law of cause and effect reigns supreme as the past experiences and present efforts of the two contestants intertwine.

NOTE
As previously noted, in the present judo structure of — kata - randori - shiai — there is no preparation for randori. There is also no preparation for shiai. The addition of beginners and recreational shiai are preparatory tools for regular shiai — present day shiai that favors the athletically inclined. These additions are to be practiced in the dojo to prepare for regular shiai. They are not substitutes for regular shiai. It is hoped with these contest preparatory additions more people will be inclined to attend shiai functions.

THE
THREE TYPES
OF
CONTEST

CONTEST
FOR
BEGINNERS

JUDO FOR EVERYONE
(BEGINNERS CONTEST CHART)
FIG 33

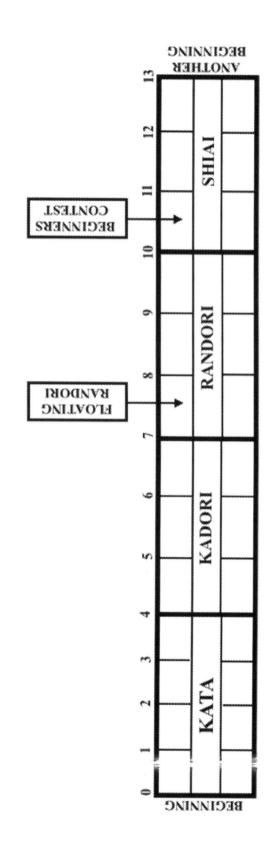

JUDO CONTESTS
FOR BEGINNERS

A) **QUALIFICATIONS TO ENTER**
   a) Able to take a break fall from a throw.
   b) Know the following techniques on both sides.
      1) Osoto-gari
      2) Ogoshi
      3) Ippon-seoi-nage
      4) Know avoidance defenses (tai-sabaki) for the above throws on both sides.
      5) Know two (2) Holding techniques.
   c) Be familiar with the IJF Contest Rules.
   d) Be familiar with the beginner kadori-shiai contest rules.

B) **BEGINNER KADORI-SHIAI CONTEST RULES**
   a) With the exception of the rules below IJF rules apply.
   b) An ippon is awarded a score of five (5) points.
   c) A waza-ari is awarded a score of four (4) points.
   d) A 10 second hold down is awarded a score of five (5) points.
   e) A contest ends after:
      1) Five (5) minutes duration
      2) One contestant scores fifteen (15) points.
   f) ONLY TAI-SABAKI defenses are allowed against throwing attacks.
   g) The first and second warnings against stiff arming or negative defending awards the non-penalized player a total of ten (10) points.
   h) The third warning against stiff arming or negative defending carries the penalty of disqualification (hansoku-make) for the penalized player.

C) **REFEREE'S COMMANDS**
   a) When a full point is awarded the referee raises one arm directly above h/her head and with all fingers and thumb extended verbally announces the score of five (5) points.
   b) When a waza-ari is awarded the referee raises one arm to the horizontal position and with four (4) fingers extended verbally announces the score of four (4) points.
   c) When the FIRST and SECOND warnings against stiff arming or negative defending is given (using the stalling signal), the referee returns the two contestants to the starting position and points to the non-penalized contender and awards h/her five (5) points EACH TIME.

d) When the third warning against stiff arming or any negative defending is given (using the stalling signal), the referee returns the two contestants to the starting position and points towards the penalized player and announces hansoku-make.

CONTEST
FOR
RECREATIONAL
PLAYERS

JUDO FOR EVERYONE
(RECREATION CONTEST CHART)
FIG 34

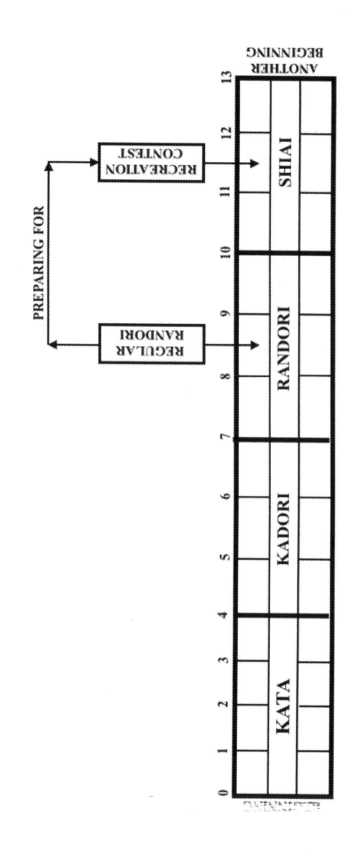

JUDO CONTESTS FOR RECREATIONAL PLAYERS

A) **QUALIFICATIONS TO ENTER**
   a) For intermediate and experienced players.
   b) Be familiar with the IJF Contest Rules.
   c) Be familiar with recreational kadori-shiai contest rules.

B) **RECREATIONAL KADORI-SHIAI CONTEST RULES**
   a) With the exception of the rules below IJF rules apply.
   b) An ippon is awarded a score of five (5) points.
   c) A waza-ari is awarded a score of four (4) points.
   d) A 10 second hold down is awarded a score of five (5) points.
   e) A submission is awarded score of fifteen (15) points.
   f) A contest ends after:
      1) A five (5) minute duration.
      2) Fifteen (15) points are scored.
   g) **ONLY TAI-SABAKI and REACTIVE HIP BLOCKING** defenses are allowed against throwing attacks.
   h) The first and second warnings against stiff arming or negative defending awards the non-penalized player a total of ten (10) points.
   i) The third warning against stiff arming or negative defending carries the penalty of disqualification (hansoku-make) for the penalized player.

C) **REFEREE'S COMMANDS**
   a) When a full point is awarded the referee raises one arm directly above h/ her head and with all fingers and thumb extended verbally announces the score of five (5) points.
   b) When a waza-ari is awarded the referee raises one arm to the horizontal position and with four (4) fingers extended verbally announces the score of four (4) points.
   c) When the FIRST and SECOND warnings against stiff arming or negative defending is given (using the stalling signal), the referee returns the two contestants to the starting position and points to the non-penalized contender and awards h/her five (5) points EACH TIME.
   d) When the third warning against stiff arming or any negative defending is given (using the stalling signal), the referee returns the two contestants to the starting position and points towards the penalized player and announces hansoku-make.

THE
ULTIMATE CONTEST
(ATHLETIC PLAYERS)

JUDO FOR EVERYONE
(THE ULTIMATE CONTEST CHART)
FIG 35

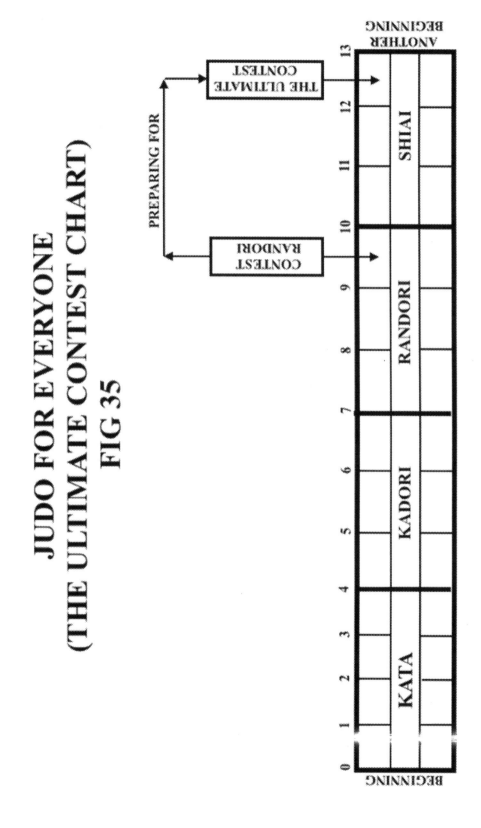

SHIAI
JUDO'S ULTIMATE TEST

A judo contest is judo practitioner's ultimate test. It consists of competitively scoring on an antagonist of equal size and experience. A score is made by successfully applying any one of judo's throwing, holding, choking or arm locking techniques. But underlying how a win is brought about is the ability to combine five things:

1) Skill, 2) Experience, 3) Fitness, 4) Fighting spirit, 5) Unpredictability.

1)   SKILL. Developing skills is an elusive enterprise because they are developed against a non-= cooperating resisting partner. When a skill works its success is obvious. But when a skill nearly works, measuring its efficacy is tricky and problematic. Skills are correctly timed coordinated movements strategically applied with power that produces a score. In the end judo skills are the fruition of years of hard work (randori and shiai) with constant reexamination and analysis (kata).

2)   EXPERIENCE. Experience is the sum total of everything a person has done. This ranges from h/her contesting, randori, coaching, and anything else that has become part of h/her judo being. Skill is what happens at a particular moment in a contest whereas experience is the subconscious guidance of all the actions that happen in a contest.

3)   FITNESS. Getting fit or very fit is not that difficult to achieve when a person practices regularly. Getting super fit is far harder and far more difficult to maintain. But if a person is serious about contesting being very fit should be looked upon as something that is just routine. It's just part of the real estate of the judo competitive world; as it is in any other physical sport. And if a contest is of special importance, being super fit should be looked upon as being a necessity.

4)   FIGHTING SPIRIT. Fighting spirit is in everyone, in many shades of gray. It's innate. It's part of the survival instinct in our species. Being enthusiastic about winning and having an innate desire to win are two different things. Everyone wants to win, otherwise why enter? But the more a person practices and the more winning becomes important the more tenacious one's fighting spirit will become.

5)   UNPREDICTABILITY. However skillful, fit and determined a person may be, unpredictability can often be the deciding factor. When a person uses familiar

gripping and attacks these are easily telegraphed and blocked; as so often happens in randori when practicing with the same partners. So unpredictability is using all that is known and using it in such a surprising way that defenses are pierced and overcome. This requires daring experimentation in randori to find out what is surprising (what works) and what turns out to be not surprising (what doesn't work).

SUMMARY
OF
JUDO FOR EVERYONE

SUMMARY

The contents of this book have attempted to explain a better way of introducing judo to beginners and improving the way judo is practiced. This is not because the present way is a dismal failure, which it obviously isn't, but because what's described on the previous pages is an improvement to what already exists. These improvements are categorized in three divisions:

1) A method of introducing beginners to the skills needed for randori — where now there is none.
2) Three choices of randori — where now there is only one.
3) Three choices of shiai — where now there is only one.

1) A method of introducing beginners to the skills needed for randori.

The method of introducing standing randori is known as: 'The Five Steps to Randori.' It serves two purposes. One, to improve beginner retention. Two, to instill the basic judo principles of harmonizing free floating movements, along with other randori skills.

BEGINNER RETENTION
Every judo instructor has experienced untold hours instructing beginners. Everything seems to go well until they have to practice standing randori, even though they may be familiar with newaza. It's at this juncture they begin to leave. Some drop out immediately and others take months or longer. Those that adjust to the rigors and challenges of standing randori usually become permanent members. Permanent as permanent can be! The five steps to randori, as explained on pages 41 to 61, gradually eases beginners into a type of standing randori — Floating Randori. However, there are no guarantees what will happen after this. But the five steps give a beginner a far greater chance of adjusting to standing randori than when h/she is just thrown cold turkey into the sink or swim pool of standing randori

BASIC JUDO PRINCIPLES
By practicing standing randori where a throwing attack is only defended against with avoidance moves(tai-sabaki), all strength against strength and wrestling type activities are removed.

See Page 136 for The Five Steps to Randori Chart.

JUDO FOR EVERYONE
(THE FIVE STEPS TO RANDORI) - FIG 36

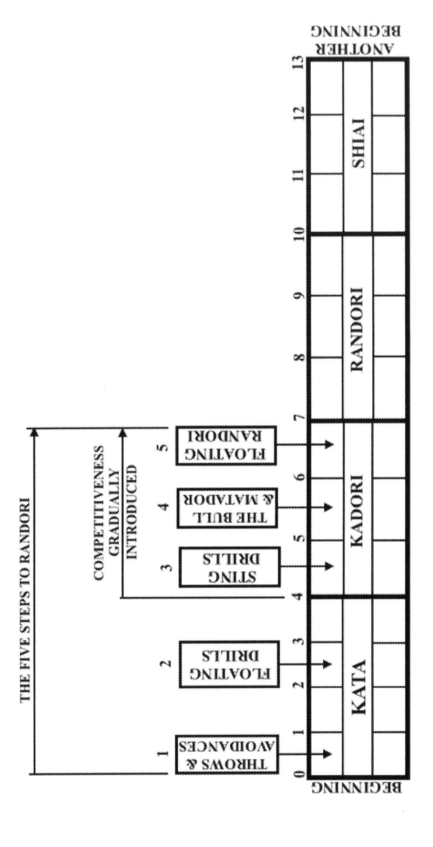

2) THREE CHOICES OF RANDORI

Presently there is only one type of randori. This one type has practice intensities that range from a kata like gentleness to the intensity of that found in shiai. Because randori practitioners usually try hard, need a lot of effort to make a throw work, and because human egos prefer to be the thrower than the one being thrown, randori, more often than not, tends to end up being like a contest. And this is fine if both partners are of like minds. But because of differences in fitness, strength, size, age, sex, mood, and ambition, it would be helpful and more user friendly if practitioners had different types of randori to choose from. Because of the above reasons the following different types of randori were created:

1) Floating Randori.

2) Regular Randori.

3) Contest Randori.

See Page 138 for The Randori Chart.

3) THREE CHOICES OF SHIAI

Presently there is only one type of contest (shiai). And to make this type of contest as fair as possible divisions are broken down by rank and weight. When they are deemed ready beginners are encouraged to compete, and naturally some to do better than others. But after the test of time three types of contestants emerge. One, the athletically inclined who are in their peak competitive years. Two, the aging recreational player who no longer has the desire or ability to compete. Three, the player who is interested, but is unable, because of family and work commitments, to practice enough. Because of the above reasons the following different types of contests were created:

1) Beginner's Contest.

2) Recreational Contest.

3) Ultimate Contest.

See Page 139 for The Shiai Chart.

JUDO FOR EVERYONE
(RANDORI CHART) – FIG 37

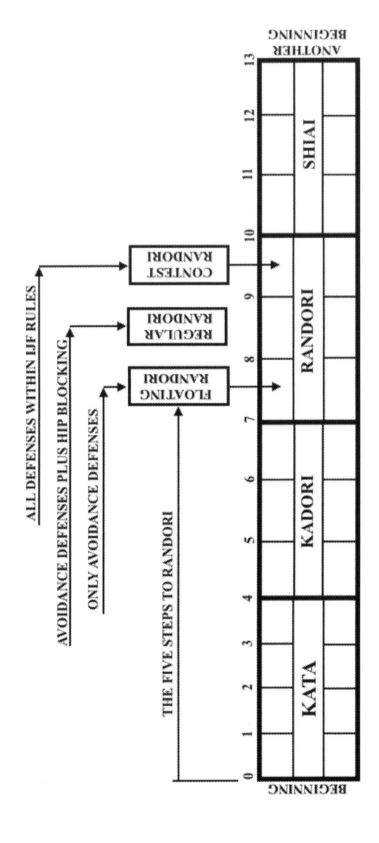

JUDO FOR EVERYONE
(SHIAI CHART) - FIG 38

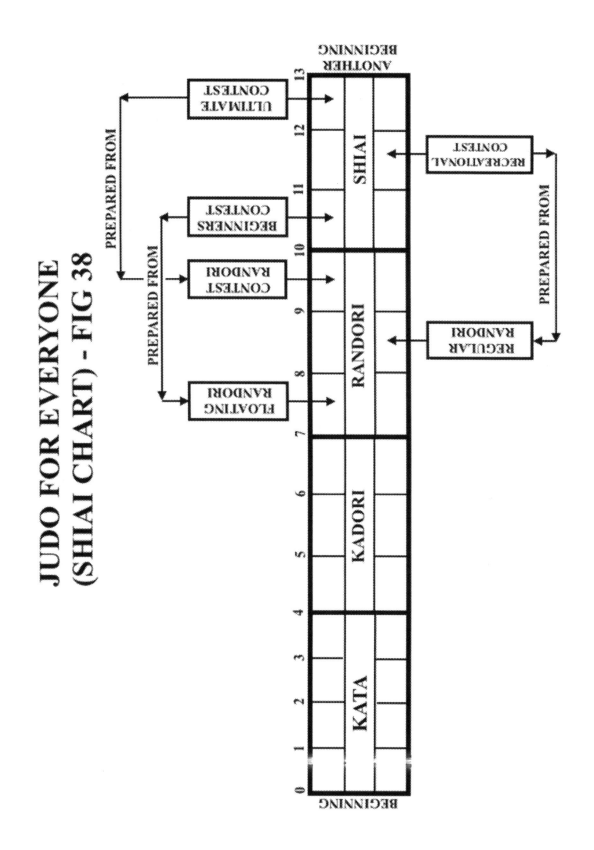

JUDO FOR EVERYONE
FIG 39

ALTERNATIVE JUDO CATEGORIES THAT ARE MORE USER FRIENDLY, EDUCATIONAL, AND FUN, FOR BOTH BEGINNERS AND EXISTING PRACTITIONERS ARE SHOWN ON THE SUMMARY CHART FIG 40

JUDO FOR EVERYONE
(SUMMARY CHART) – FIG 40

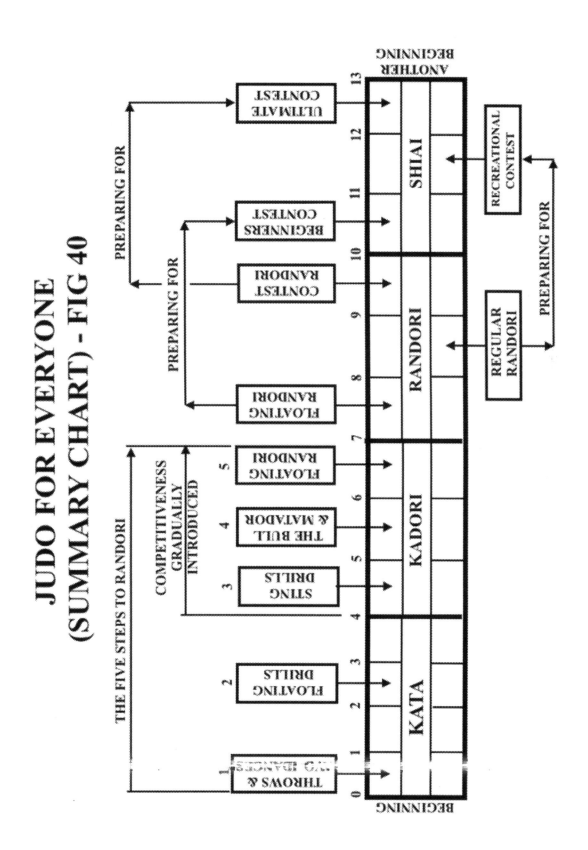

CLOSING NOTES

CLOSING NOTES

NOTE - 1

The alternate categories are not intended to change judo in any way. Judo is judo and the new categories do not and cannot change this. The new categories are to help the judo of beginners and seasoned practitioners alike. Once beginners have adapted to the practice of randori it's still hard work. But the five steps adapt them to the enjoyable hard work of randori that is challenging, thought provoking, and has extremely rewarding physical and mental health benefits. It is hoped that the new categories will appeal to a wider audience than just the athletically inclined, reduce drop-out rates, instill judo skills from the get-go, and improve the enjoyment of judo through the increased choices offered in the new types of randori and shiai.

NOTE - 2

The three categories of judo — kata - randori - shiai — served judo well during the 19th and 20th centuries but the circumstances for their use in the 21st century is now different.

During the 19th century when judo was founded, judo was, and still is, practiced in Japanese high schools and other institutions where there is an endless supply of students. This supply rotates every four years. First year students come in (beginners) and at the end of the fourth -year seasoned students go out. It didn't matter if they enjoyed or hated judo. They did four years and the transition from kata to randori worked because they couldn't leave. They were a captured audience that practiced judo every day of the school year for four school years. It didn't matter how efficient or inefficient the system was it was bound to produce some fantastic players over the four years. Which resulted in the unspoken conclusion that the system obviously worked.

During the first half and more of the 20th century, when judo spread throughout the world, judo was the only kid on the block — as previously mentioned, there was no Bruce Lee, Gracie Ju-jitsu and MMA around at that time. During this period the system that obviously worked in Japan was again used, but the difference was students were no longer a captive audience — they could leave if they didn't like what they were doing. How many millions left judo after not being able to adjust to the kata randori transition will never be known.

In the 21st century the forces of the free market are at work and people have choices and they are not choosing judo. The law of evolution proves that if something, whether it be a specie, a business, a style, an idea or a sport, does not adapt to its environment, it becomes extinct. So, for judo to survive it has to be more user friendly for new people trying it out and make judo more user friendly for these new people when they are past the beginner's stage and are regular practitioners. Hence the five steps to randori (formerly Kelly's Capers), and the addition of two more types of user friendly randori and shiai.

NOTE - 3

To attain the best results from introducing the five steps it is imperative that beginners do not mix their five step randori with any other type of randori. If they become involved with a randori, especially on a regular basis, that consists of struggling, stiffness, strength against strength wrestling type actions, activities where defending takes precedence over attacking, and winning or one-up man ship is a priority, the beginner will be drawn into the same old same old. This is especially true in the first six months or so, because in the beginning might is right. Without having skillful movements to defend against a throwing attack it is so easy to move a pair of stiff arms a few inches, and sometimes even less, to block a throw. And from this same old same old nothing is learned. If a beginner is trying to use what he was taught — the five steps — and the other person is practicing a fighting randori which h/she developed from the usual kata — randori introduction, the beginner will get frustrated, and either leave after a short while, or, use might and fight back and lose h/her development of free floating movements. If a beginner finds h/she enjoys the challenge of a fighting type randori h/she will probably stay a while. If not h/she will leave.

The way to get around this is for everyone who is practicing with a beginner should practice with the beginner the same way the beginner is practicing. And the way to do this is simply have everyone in the class be familiar with the five steps to randori. Example 1: If a beginner has completed only stage one of the five steps — ogoshi, osoto-gari, ippon-seoi-nage, and their avoidance defenses — then whoever is practicing with the beginner should only use these throws and avoidances and freely allow the beginner to attack. Example 2: If a beginner has only completed part of stage two and only knows hiza-guruma and kouchi-gari and their avoidances of stage two, then whoever is practicing with the beginner should only use the throws ogoshi, osoto-gari, ippon-seoi-nage, hiza-guruma, kouchi-gari and their avoidance defenses and freely allow the beginner to attack. So before a practice the higher grade should ask the beginner what throws he knows from the five steps and adjust accordingly. After practicing with the beginner h/she can revert back to practicing with more experienced players however hard h/she wants to. By having three choices of practice, instead of one, it is far easier for partners to adjust to each-others skill levels, thus making a randori session more enjoyable for the whole class.

With such progressive practices the beginner will feel comfortable when practicing randori which will greatly increase the chances that the h/she will remain in judo and become a regular practicing member. From here a beginner can more easily acclimate him/herself to the more competitive forms of randori — regular randori, and contest randori (shidori).

ABOUT THE AUTHOR

Sid Kelly worked as an engineer for fifty-five years designing high speed automation assembly machines and production equipment — pens, razors, lighters, glass and medical equipment and more.

For over sixty years, he has practiced, competed, studied, and written about the martial art of sport judo. He was in the British judo squad and represented Great Britain on nine occasions in international matches (1965-67). He was head instructor of the Renrukan JC that produced three British Team players. He captained the Northern Home Counties (NHC) team winning the Area Team Championships (1966), and won Britain's first kata championship at the NHC Area Championships (1965), and passed the National Coach Award Examination first time.

Sid emigrated to the USA in 1967. He was overall winner of the New England Black Belt championships, two times Connecticut State Champion. He was owner and head instructor of a judo and karate school for 10 years that had 200 + members. He was an active national referee for ten years. He produced three videos (70 applications of the arm lock Waki-gatame)(1990-1995), and five videos (multi-choice testing on 110 techniques)(1995-1996). He was two times gold medalist in the Worlds Masters Judo Championships (Canada 1999) (Japan 2004), and coached the winning Connecticut Judo Team in the United States Judo Association (USJA) National Team Championships (1999). October 16th was declared SID KELLY DAY in appreciation of his judo services to the town of Milford, Ct. (1999). He was awarded the rank of 8th degree black belt (2005). Certified as a personal trainer, Certified USJA Coach, Certified Master Examiner, and Certified Kata Examiner. Chairman of the USJA Promotion Board (2008-2013) — rewriting and updating the USJA Promotion Manual. For thirty-five years he was on the teaching staff at Americas oldest judo camp — the NY YMCA International Judo Camp. Published 'Judo Poems' (2009). Created, tested, and copyrighted a system that introduces new students to the skills needed to competitively apply throwing techniques (the 5 steps to standing randori) (2010 - 2018). Created 3 types of standing practices (randori) and 3 types of judo contests: for beginners, recreational players and the athletically inclined (2018).

In retirement he gives judo clinics, reads, writes, teaches English as a second language, belongs to a health club, and attends a writing club.

He lives with his wife Rita in West Haven, Ct, USA. They have two children, Susan and Tom, and three grandsons, Beau, Atticus, and Thaddeus.

Printed in the United States
By Bookmasters